The Advent of
RESCUE

2024 Advent Reflections
based on The Rescue Project

The Advent of Rescue
2024 Companion Guide based on The Rescue Project
ACTS XXIX, Copyright © 2024. All rights reserved.

Cover: *The Annunciation* (1898), Henry Ossawa Tanner (1859-1937), Philadelphia Museum of Art, Philadelphia, PA

https://www.actsxxix.org
https://rescueproject.us

Daily Reflections: Sister Teresa Harrell, Society of Mary

ISBN: 979-8-9897270-1-8

Library of Congress Control Number: 2024908950

Printed in the United States of America

XXIX
PRESS

Published by ACTS XXIX Press
38695 Seven Mile Road, Suite 110
Livonia, Michigan 48152
actsxxix.org | press@actsxxix.org

A FRIEND IS ON THE WAY

FR. JOHN RICCARDO

"This is the day. The invasion has begun!"

nne Frank wrote those words in her Diary on June 6, 1944. That was the day, of course, that the Allies landed on the beaches of Normandy and turned the tide of World War II. Frank went on to write, "Is this really the liberation we've all talked so much about, which still seems too good, too much of a fairy tale ever to come true?...The best part of the invasion is that I have the feeling that friends are on the way...The thought of friends and salvation means everything to us!"

Similar words—"invasion," "liberation," "salvation"—could have been written by another young girl nearly two thousand years earlier. That young girl, of course, was Mary, who was roughly the same age as Anne Frank.

C.S. Lewis, a contemporary of Frank, drew heavily on the imagery from World War II and the Allies landing to help explain what is called the Incarnation, that is, God becoming Flesh in the Person of Jesus. In his classic work *Mere Christianity*, Lewis writes, "Enemy-occupied territory—that is what this world is. Christianity is the story of how the rightful king has landed, you might say landed in disguise...God has landed on this enemy-occupied world in human form." Perhaps we could put all of this together and say that the Incarnation of the Eternal Son of God is the invasion of one kingdom—the kingdom of Sin, of Death and of Satan—by another and stronger kingdom—the Kingdom of God. And all of this happened for each one of us by name.

This extraordinary, incredible, hopeful, life-changing news lies at the heart of the Gospel message and at the heart of the season of Advent.

For many years, I personally found Advent a very challenging season. Most of us have some sense of what Lent is about—an extended time of prayerful and penitential purification so as to get ready to celebrate Jesus' triumphant resurrection. Most of us have at least some basic idea what we're supposed to do during those 40 days. But what about Advent? What are we supposed to do in these days, except decorate the house, get ready to host family and friends, and above all, shop for Christmas? Are we preparing to celebrate the Lord's birth, His second coming, both, or something else entirely?

The readings at Mass, up until the final days before Christmas, draw our attention to how the Lord God is going to bring about a definitive restoration to His very good creation. We know that something is wrong with the world, that things are not as they should be, and yet we don't see any way out—at least not on our own. In that respect, our race before the Incarnation of the Lord Jesus was like the people of Europe in World War II. Ever since that fateful day in Eden so long ago, the human race had been held bound by the tyranny of Sin, Death and a foe far more terrifying than Hitler or the

Nazi war machine. Ours was a race that had been held in slavery to powers we could never escape from or defeat on our own. Sin and Death are spoken of in Scripture not just as things that we do or that will happen to us—they are these, of course. But Scripture speaks of them as though they are governments, dominions, enemy armies that we cannot defeat on our own. They captured us when our first parents back in the Garden believed the lie that forever tempts us even today: "God is not a good Father. You can't trust Him. You can be happier apart from Him." Without knowing what they were doing, our first parents unknowingly sold our race into slavery to these powers and there was no way out on our own. And ever since then, despite all the many great achievements and accomplishments of our race, we've been forever haunted and hunted by Death.

However, the Scriptures in these Advent days turn our attention to various prophecies in the Old Testament of an unforeseen breakthrough, a making right of things gone wrong, an unimaginable end to Death and the one who tyrannizes us. The Gospel passages in these days show us Jesus inaugurating and fulfilling the many things that had been prophesied so many years before, and exhorting us to prepare for His triumphant return when He will both render judgment and definitively make all things new. In the last days before the celebration of the Nativity of our Lord Jesus, we linger with the wondrous events of the annunciation to Mary and to Zechariah; Joseph's sudden shock at his beloved's pregnancy, followed by the angel's instruction about the origin of the Child; Mary's visit to Elizabeth, and finally the birth of the King who has "landed in disguise."

I would suggest the joy and hope we hear in Anne Frank's words are the model for us as we ponder anew all that we're about to celebrate.

Is it "too much of a fairy tale" to believe that you matter to God? That you're worth the trouble of God becoming man? That you are worth dying for to the One through whom and for whom all things were created? That God calls you His friend?

No. It's all true. You do matter to God! You are worth the trouble of God becoming man! You are worth dying for to God! He does call you friend!

This is why the gospel is good news. Not just news. Good news. Extraordinary news. Unimaginable news. Life changing news.

What is the logical, rational, intelligent response to such extraordinary acts of love? Isn't it to trust in God? Isn't it to love Him? Isn't it to praise and adore Him? Isn't it to say, just like Mary to the angel, "Fiat! Be it done to me according to your word!"

In a time when lasting hope, joy, and encouragement are in short supply, let us focus our attention in these days on the One who holds all things in His hands, who is the Author of history (His-story), who loves us beyond all telling, and who has come to fight for us.

INTRODUCTION

In our anxious American culture, we can forget all about Advent. It's easy to get caught up in the swirl of holiday parties, decorating, shopping, baking, and trying to please everyone on your gift list. Rather than a time of quiet, expectant hope—a time of deeper prayer, a time of gentle penance in preparation for the coming of the Savior—this season has become a time of frantic desperation and restlessness, a time of indulgence and overspending, a time of stressful overplanning.

It's a great loss when we lose this season, because when we lose Advent, we lose Christmas. And if we lose Christmas, we lose touch with the most essential truths about who we are created to be, how we became enslaved, and all that the God of the universe has done to rescue us from that slavery. We forget the reason we are celebrating, forget what Christmas is, forget who Jesus is, forget what He has done for us.

Remembering is imperative. Unless we remember, we become dismembered, scattered, pulled in every direction, driven by the changing winds of our culture, unmoored from the deepest truths of our identity. Unless we remember, Christmas becomes just another consumer-culture holiday, all about buying and getting. Unless we remember, we are cut off from the reality of what happened some 2024 years ago, in Bethlehem of Judea.

This Advent meditation booklet is designed to help us slow down for a moment each day, to remember again who Jesus is, who we are, and why He came for us, to prepare our hearts for the celebration of Christmas. It follows the kerygma, the essential proclamation of our faith: that we were created in God's image and likeness; that we have been captured by a powerful Enemy; that the Son of God became incarnate in the person of Jesus Christ, who was born, lived, suffered, died, and rose again to rescue us and bring us new life; that we are called to respond to Him with our lives. Each meditation will connect to some aspect of this kerygma, tying it in to the readings of that day.

The format is simple: we provide readings for the day and then a simple meditation on one of those readings, connecting it to the kerygma, and finally suggest some questions to pray with and an action to do so that what we pray will transform us.

We invite you to enter into this season with a spirit of hope and expectation, to come to your daily meditation on Scripture with expectancy and openness, confident that the Lord is going to speak to you, that the Holy Spirit will open up the Word of God to you in a new way, that through this time of prayer with Scripture, the God who loves you is going to be continuing His work of salvation in you.

Some Tips for Prayer

It's helpful to prepare a place for your prayer, if you are not praying in a chapel or church before the Blessed Sacrament. Try to have the same place every day, a kind of permanent "prayer corner" in your room or in your home, with a small "altar" where you have a crucifix or image of Jesus, an image of Our Lady, a candle, and your Bible.

Invoke the Holy Spirit to begin your time of prayer. The same Holy Spirit who inspired the writing of each word of the Bible wants to come to you and open up the Scriptures to you, but He always waits for the invitation. So spend some time invoking the Holy Spirit, asking Him to open the Scriptures to you and open you to the Scriptures.

Pray the short Advent prayer provided below.

Slowly read the daily readings in your own Bible, and spend a few moments pondering them.

Then read the provided meditation, and pray with each of the questions provided at the end.

Finally, write down any insights or lights from this time of prayer in your spiritual journal, whatever the Lord spoke to you, and include an evaluation of your prayer (if you were distracted and by what, if you experienced that it was easy to pray or what caused difficulties, etc.). Then end with an Our Father, a Hail Mary, and a Glory Be.

Advent Prayer

Lord my God, this is the season of Advent, the season of expecting You to come. So I ask You to come to me this morning, as I begin this time of meditation on Your Word. Make my heart a place of stillness and receptivity, like the heart of Mary, who was able to receive You in her body and in her soul. Let whatever I meditate this morning grow inside of me, as You grew inside of her. Eternal Word of God, please become incarnate in me again, through this time of prayer, transforming me to live in the new life You came to bring me. I give You permission to change me, to convert me, to live Your life in me. Like Mary, I say to you, "Let it be done to me "

WEEK ONE

CREATED

This first week of Advent, the Lord invites us to meditate on the reality of creation, that He is the Creator of all this vast universe and of each one of us, that He has created us in love and for love, and that He wants to provide for us all that we need. It is a week to return to wonder: at the vastness of creation, at the goodness and nearness of our Creator, at our own selves, created in His image. Let's enter into this week with a great openness, so that the Lord can tell us anew how good it is that we exist, how good it is that we are human, and how great is the calling He has for us.

SUNDAY, DECEMBER 1

"There will be signs in the sun, the moon, and the stars."

A reading from the Book of Jeremiah (33:14-16)

The days are coming, says the LORD,
  when I will fulfill the promise
  I made to the house of Israel and Judah.
In those days, in that time,
  I will raise up for David a just shoot ;
  he shall do what is right and just in the land.
In those days Judah shall be safe
  and Jerusalem shall dwell secure;
  this is what they shall call her:
  "The LORD our justice."

Responsorial Psalm (25:4-5, 8-9, 10, 14)

R. **To you, O Lord, I lift my soul.**

Your ways, O LORD, make known to me;
  teach me your paths,
Guide me in your truth and teach me,
  for you are God my savior,
  and for you I wait all the day. R.

Good and upright is the LORD;
  thus he shows sinners the way.
He guides the humble to justice,
  and teaches the humble his way. R.

All the paths of the LORD are kindness and constancy
  toward those who keep his covenant and his decrees.
The friendship of the LORD is with those who fear him,
  and his covenant, for their instruction. R.

Brothers and sisters:
May the Lord make you increase and abound in love
for one another and for all,
just as we have for you,
so as to strengthen your hearts,
to be blameless in holiness before our God and Father
at the coming of our Lord Jesus with all his holy ones.
    Amen.

Finally, brothers and sisters,
we earnestly ask and exhort you in the Lord Jesus
    that,
as you received from us
how you should conduct yourselves to please God
—and as you are conducting yourselves—
you do so even more.
For you know what instructions we gave you through
    the Lord Jesus.

Jesus said to his disciples:
"There will be signs in the sun, the moon, and the stars,
and on earth nations will be in dismay,
perplexed by the roaring of the sea and the waves.
People will die of fright
in anticipation of what is coming upon the world,
for the powers of the heavens will be shaken.
And then they will see the Son of Man
coming in a cloud with power and great glory.
But when these signs begin to happen,
stand erect and raise your heads
because your redemption is at hand.

"Beware that your hearts do not become drowsy
from carousing and drunkenness
and the anxieties of daily life,
and that day catch you by surprise like a trap.
For that day will assault everyone
who lives on the face of the earth.
Be vigilant at all times
and pray that you have the strength
to escape the tribulations that are imminent
and to stand before the Son of Man."

The other day at lunch, several of us were speaking about works of literature, sharing the wonder of how one word can convey so much meaning, how there can be so much more in each sentence than first meets the eye, and how the same is true in Scripture, layers of meaning, richness waiting for us to delve in and discover hidden treasures. But it's not just written works that speak, that convey meaning. The Psalmist tells us that the heavens proclaim God's glory, that every day and night they speak a message.

And when we read the first chapter of Genesis, we understand something profound about creation: God spoke it into being. And the first chapter of John's Gospel tells us that all things were created through the Word of God.

The eternal Word of God cannot speak something meaningless or purposeless. No, every word that God speaks is full of meaning, and thus everything in all of creation is full of meaning, telling us something about our Creator. We keep discovering that the universe is bigger and bigger than we'd ever imagined, full of more stars and planets and galaxies than we could ever have guessed. What does that tell us about our Creator? Because everything in the universe is what it is and points to something else, to Someone else, to the great Creator, who thought each thing, designed each thing, spoke each thing into being, and continues to hold it in being. So everything speaks, everything tells us something, everything bears a message, and we are called, as those created in God's image and likeness, to discover the message.

It's worth our while to return to wonder, to marvel at the majesty of the mountains, to look up at the stars, more numerous than we can count, in our own galaxy and realize that what we can see is just one tiny fraction of the universe, to be overcome with awe at the vastness of creation. It's worth our while to sit and contemplate the waves crashing on the beach, the enduring patience and persistence of the ocean. It's worth our while to delight in the sparrow's song and the lofty flight of the eagle. It's worth our while to be still and know that He is God, that we are not, and that He is constantly speaking to us, making Himself known, through this vast creation that He holds in His hands.

And that itself tells us enough to ponder for days—He holds this whole universe and every detail of it in His eternal hands, and nothing, not even a single grain of sand, can slip through His fingers. So we can rest (at least for some minutes) today, and let go of all the things that worry us, all the ways we feel we need to be in control. We can just be the beloved creatures that we are, delighting in the greatness and beauty of this vast creation, being still and knowing that He is God and that we are His.

Questions for reflection:

1.   *What in this universe most fills you with awe or wonder? Why? What is that telling you about the Creator?*

2.   *When was the last time you delighted in some aspect of creation? What was it? What did it tell you about God?*

3.   *What things in creation most clearly speak to you of God? What do they tell you?*

Action: Today, spend at least five minutes doing nothing beside contemplating something in creation.

Advent will conclude, of course, with the Solemnity of the birth of the Lord Jesus. However, there's often not a lot of clarity on the reason why the eternal Son of God became flesh, born of the Virgin Mary. What exactly was the mission of Jesus? The Sundays of Advent are a wonderful opportunity to help a parish better understand Jesus' mission, and to bring everyone along on a sort of extended retreat in preparation for Christmas.

What is offered below is a suggestion for how a priest or deacon may choose to preach the kerygma in these holy weeks with this goal in mind. **The suggestions are based on *The Rescue Project*, which we strongly recommend parishes consult as they move through Advent** (rescueproject.us). Each week breaks open one of four "big questions" that lie at the heart of *The Rescue Project*, and be helpful in understanding both the story of salvation history in general and the kerygma in particular:

1. Why is there something rather than nothing?
2. Why is everything so obviously messed up?
3. What, if anything, has God done about it? And
4. How should I respond?

These four "big questions" can be simplified to four words:

1. Created
2. Captured
3. Rescued
4. Response

May we all be overwhelmed in the days ahead by what the Lord has done for us! May we be moved by the Holy Spirit to surrender ourselves more fully to God! And may we be mobilized for mission to go and evangelize and recreate this world that God loves so much that He sent His only Son.

1st Sunday of Advent
Part One: Created

Ask God for the grace of wonder and trust

Key Themes: Any of these are worth exploring this week. The key is to ask the Lord what is most significant for your particular community!

- There is only one God.

- He chose freely and out of love to create everything that is.

- Everything He created is good.

- The highlight of His creation is the human person, made in His image and likeness.

- We have been created with reason and freedom, which enable us to love.

- We were created out of love to be loved and to love.

- Our ultimate destiny is to be divinized (cf. 2 Peter 1:4).

- God is more powerful than anything or anyone we can conceive.

Questions for Reflection:

- What is my image of God? Where did that image come from?

- Do I live life confident in God's love for me personally or do I live in fear and anxiety?

- What am I anxious or fearful about right now in my life?

- As I contemplate the grandeur of the universe that God created and His love for me by name, how do those things affect my fears and anxiety?

Possible Verses for Focus from Today's Readings:

Jeremiah (33:14-16): "The days are coming, says the LORD, when I will fulfill the promise. I made to the house of Israel and Judah. In those days, in that time, I will raise up for David a just shoot; he shall do what is right and just in the land. In those days Judah shall be safe and Jerusalem shall dwell secure; this is what they shall call her: 'The LORD our justice.'"

[What promise? New creation, restoration, a new exodus, and a new covenant—and not just for the houses of Israel and Judah but all people.]

Luke (21:27-28): "And then they will see the Son of Man coming in a cloud with power and great glory. But when these signs begin to happen, stand erect and raise your heads because your redemption is at hand."

[Though we may often mistakenly think this, when the Son of Man returns it will not be to take us away but to make all things new.]

NOTES

NOTES

MONDAY, DECEMBER 2
"Come, let us walk in the light of the Lord!"

A reading from the Book of the Prophet Isaiah (2:1-5)

This is what Isaiah, son of Amoz,
   saw concerning Judah and Jerusalem.

In days to come,
The mountain of the LORD's house
shall be established as the highest mountain
and raised above the hills.
All nations shall stream toward it;
many peoples shall come and say:
"Come, let us climb the LORD's mountain,
to the house of the God of Jacob,
That he may instruct us in his ways,
and we may walk in his paths."
For from Zion shall go forth instruction,
and the word of the LORD from Jerusalem.
He shall judge between the nations,
and impose terms on many peoples.
They shall beat their swords into plowshares
and their spears into pruning hooks;
One nation shall not raise the sword against another,
nor shall they train for war again.

O house of Jacob, come,
let us walk in the light of the LORD!

Responsorial Psalm (122:1-2, 3-4b, 4cd-5, 6-7, 8-9)

R. **Let us go rejoicing to the house of the Lord.**

I rejoiced because they said to me,
   "We will go up to the house of the LORD."

And now we have set foot
within your gates, O Jerusalem. R.

Jerusalem, built as a city
with compact unity.
To it the tribes go up,
the tribes of the LORD. R.

According to the decree for Israel,
to give thanks to the name of the LORD.
In it are set up judgment seats,
seats for the house of David. R.

Pray for the peace of Jerusalem!
May those who love you prosper!
May peace be within your walls,
prosperity in your buildings. R.

Because of my relatives and friends
I will say, "Peace be within you!"
Because of the house of the LORD, our God,
I will pray for your good. R.

A reading from the holy Gospel according to Matthew
(8:5-11)

When Jesus entered Capernaum,
a centurion approached him and appealed to him,
saying,
"Lord, my servant is lying at home paralyzed, suffering dreadfully."
He said to him, "I will come and cure him."
The centurion said in reply,
"Lord, I am not worthy to have you enter under my roof;
only say the word and my servant will be healed.
For I too am a man subject to authority,
with soldiers subject to me.

And I say to one, 'Go,' and he goes;
and to another, 'Come here,' and he comes;
and to my slave, 'Do this,' and he does it."
When Jesus heard this, he was amazed and said to
those following him,
"Amen, I say to you, in no one in Israel have I found
such faith.
I say to you, many will come from the east and the
west,
and will recline with Abraham, Isaac, and Jacob
at the banquet in the Kingdom of heaven."

One of the most moving lines in the first three chapters
of Genesis is in chapter 3, where it says that God is walking in the garden in the breezy time of the day. I've always
imagined that, prior to the Fall, Adam and Eve walked with
God each evening, before the sun set, as the day cooled,
and in that moment of intimacy with Him, shared with Him
what they had lived that day, letting Him shine His light on
all their experiences. And in His light, they could see the
full truth of what they had lived, the full truth of their own
identity, the full truth of who He is.

To walk in the light of the Lord is to walk in the light of
His love for us. Yes, you and I are created out of the
dust of the Earth, one of nine planets in our solar system, which is one of 3,916 solar systems in our Milky
Way galaxy, which is one of more than 200 billion galaxies in the known universe, which is 93 billion light years
across. And, yes, maybe it seems absurd that we could
even matter at all to the Creator of all this vast universe.

But, absurd or not, it's true. The Creator of this universe
doesn't just hold the universe in His hands. He holds me

in His hands. He holds *you* in His hands. For some inexplicable reason, you and I *matter* to Him. What you and I do *interests* Him. No detail of our lives, of our days, is to Him indifferent. He *cares* for us.

He cares so much that He wants to have time with us each day, to walk with us in the garden of our lives, to listen to us as we open our hearts to Him, to shine the light of His loving truth on each experience of our day, each experience of our lives. The light He wants to shine every day is the light of the truth that He, the Creator of this vast and wondrous universe, is also our Creator, that we are His specially loved creatures, adopted as His *children*.

So come, let us walk in the light of the Lord, the light of His love, and let Him show us who He is and who we are for Him.

Questions for reflection:

1. *In what ways have you allowed the Lord to shine the light of His love into your life? What has His light revealed to you?*

2. *When you have taken the time to speak with the Lord about your day at the end of the day, what have you seen more clearly about the events of the day?*

3. *How have you experienced that you, personally, matter to God?*

Action: Set aside 10 minutes at the end of your day today, to perhaps go for a walk and speak with the Lord about everything you've lived this day.

TUESDAY, DECEMBER 3
*"There shall be no harm or ruin
on all my holy mountain."*

A reading from the Book of the Prophet Isaiah (11:1-10)

On that day,
A shoot shall sprout from the stump of Jesse,
and from his roots a bud shall blossom.
The Spirit of the LORD shall rest upon him:
a Spirit of wisdom and of understanding,
A Spirit of counsel and of strength,
a Spirit of knowledge and of fear of the LORD,
and his delight shall be the fear of the LORD.
Not by appearance shall he judge,
nor by hearsay shall he decide,
But he shall judge the poor with justice,
and decide aright for the land's afflicted.
He shall strike the ruthless with the rod of his mouth,
and with the breath of his lips he shall slay the wicked.
Justice shall be the band around his waist,
and faithfulness a belt upon his hips.

Then the wolf shall be a guest of the lamb,
and the leopard shall lie down with the kid;
The calf and the young lion shall browse together,
with a little child to guide them.
The cow and the bear shall be neighbors,
together their young shall rest;
the lion shall eat hay like the ox.
The baby shall play by the cobra's den,
and the child lay his hand on the adder's lair.
There shall be no harm or ruin on all my holy mountain;
for the earth shall be filled with knowledge of the LORD,
as water covers the sea.

On that day,
The root of Jesse,
set up as a signal for the nations,
The Gentiles shall seek out,
for his dwelling shall be glorious.

Responsorial Psalm (72:1-2, 7-8, 12-13, 17)

R. **Justice shall flourish in his time, and fullness of peace forever.**

O God, with your judgment endow the king,
and with your justice, the king's son;
He shall govern your people with justice
and your afflicted ones with judgment. R.

Justice shall flower in his days,
and profound peace, till the moon be no more.
May he rule from sea to sea,
and from the River to the ends of the earth. R.

He shall rescue the poor when he cries out,
and the afflicted when he has no one to help him.
He shall have pity for the lowly and the poor;
the lives of the poor he shall save. R.

May his name be blessed forever;
as long as the sun his name shall remain.
In him shall all the tribes of the earth be blessed;
all the nations shall proclaim his happiness. R.

A reading from the holy Gospel according to Luke
(10:21-24)

Jesus rejoiced in the Holy Spirit and said,
"I give you praise, Father, Lord of heaven and earth,
for although you have hidden these things

from the wise and the learned
you have revealed them to the childlike.
Yes, Father, such has been your gracious will.
All things have been handed over to me by my Father.
No one knows who the Son is except the Father,
and who the Father is except the Son
and anyone to whom the Son wishes to reveal him."

Turning to the disciples in private he said,
"Blessed are the eyes that see what you see.
For I say to you,
many prophets and kings desired to see what you see,
but did not see it,
and to hear what you hear, but did not hear it."

Try for a moment to imagine the world as Isaiah describes it: the wolf as the guest of the lamb; the calf and the young lion browsing together, guided by a little child; the cow and bear lying down to rest together, no possible harm, even from the cobra; no harm or ruin on all the earth.

It's hard for us to believe, this side of Eden, but that's how things were supposed to be; that's the world as created by God: no death, no suffering, no harm, no killing, no violence of any kind anywhere in creation. We were created, all things were created, to be in harmony with God and with one another.

Harmony: that's an apt word for God's design. Each creature has a specific note to sing, and the blending of all things was to create a beautiful symphony, played at all times and in all places, nothing discordant, no false notes, nothing flat or sharp, all in perfect harmony.

And our role, as humans, aware of this Divine plan—aware of our relationship with God, with one another, and with the world around us—was to knowingly sing and play our part.

Although we are small, our part is not unimportant. Made in God's image and likeness, we are to spread—through our actions and our words—knowledge of God through all the earth. We are created to show the rest of creation who and how God is. It's a great mission, one that's bigger than us, for sure, but one for which Adam and Eve had all the grace they needed from God.

And that's what they did, for a time, in Eden, governing and guiding all the other creatures to live in harmony. Let's stay for a moment there, in our imagination, in the world Isaiah describes, the world that Adam and Eve inhabited. Let's see the beauty and the goodness of God's creation, so that we can come to love it more now, as it is today. And let's ask for the grace to live in harmony now, with Him first, so that we can live in harmony with the rest of this beautiful world that He so dearly loves.

Questions for reflection:

1. *What is your first response or reaction to the idea that God created all things to live in harmony, with no killing or harm? Why is that your response?*

2. *If human beings are the ones who tell the rest of the world who and how God is, what does your life currently say about God?*

3. *Why do you think God so loves this world?*

Action: Spend some time out in nature today, in some way, contemplating the beauty of creation around you. (If you live in a city, spend some time in a yard or a park.) Give thanks to God for all the harmony you see even now.

A reading from the Book of the Prophet Isaiah (25:6-10a)

On this mountain the LORD of hosts
will provide for all peoples
A feast of rich food and choice wines,
juicy, rich food and pure, choice wines.
On this mountain he will destroy
the veil that veils all peoples,
The web that is woven over all nations;
he will destroy death forever.
The Lord GOD will wipe away
the tears from all faces;
The reproach of his people he will remove
from the whole earth; for the LORD has spoken.

On that day it will be said:
"Behold our God, to whom we looked to save us!
This is the LORD for whom we looked;
let us rejoice and be glad that he has saved us!"
For the hand of the LORD will rest on this mountain.

Responsorial Psalm (23:1-3a, 3b-4, 5, 6)

R. **I shall live in the house of the Lord all the days of
my life.**

The LORD is my shepherd; I shall not want.
In verdant pastures he gives me repose;
Beside restful waters he leads me;
he refreshes my soul. R.

He guides me in right paths
for his name's sake.

Even though I walk in the dark valley
I fear no evil; for you are at my side
With your rod and your staff
that give me courage. R.

 You spread the table before me
in the sight of my foes;
You anoint my head with oil;
my cup overflows. R.

Only goodness and kindness follow me
all the days of my life;
And I shall dwell in the house of the LORD
for years to come. R.

A reading from the holy Gospel according to Matthew
(15:29-37)

At that time:
Jesus walked by the Sea of Galilee,
went up on the mountain, and sat down there.
Great crowds came to him,
having with them the lame, the blind, the deformed,
    the mute,
and many others.
They placed them at his feet, and he cured them.
The crowds were amazed when they saw the mute
    speaking,
the deformed made whole,
the lame walking,
and the blind able to see,
and they glorified the God of Israel.

Jesus summoned his disciples and said,
"My heart is moved with pity for the crowd,
for they have been with me now for three days

and have nothing to eat.
I do not want to send them away hungry,
for fear they may collapse on the way."
The disciples said to him,
"Where could we ever get enough bread in this de-
serted place
to satisfy such a crowd?"
Jesus said to them, "How many loaves do you have?"
"Seven," they replied, "and a few fish."
He ordered the crowd to sit down on the ground.
Then he took the seven loaves and the fish,
gave thanks, broke the loaves,
and gave them to the disciples, who in turn gave them
to the crowds.
They all ate and were satisfied.
They picked up the fragments left over—seven
baskets full.

In the beginning, when God created the world and created Adam and Eve, He placed them in the Garden of
Eden. Eden is a sign of God's perfect providence—they
lack no good thing and have abundant resources within
reach. He provides for them all that they need and even
all they could legitimately want. "You are free to eat," the
Lord tells them, "from any of the trees of the garden,
except the tree of the knowledge of good and evil."

You are free to eat from any of the trees of the garden.
You didn't till it, didn't plant it, didn't water it, but you can
eat of it. I did it all for you, prepared it all for you. You lack
nothing you could need. And now you can participate in
My work, now that the garden is planted and grown for you
and you are here, you can tend to it, since work is good for
you. And you can eat from any of the trees. Whatever you
want or need, whenever you want or need it.

That's the generosity of God, who provides for all we need, more abundantly than we could even think to imagine.

We were created to depend on God and to trust in His providence, the loving providence of the God who is our Father, who created us out of love, who provides for us out of love, who knows what is good for us, who always has had in mind all that we need, and who will, if we let Him, provide exactly what we need when we need it. We do not need to grasp, to take for ourselves. We need only to open our hands and let Him fill them.

Whatever you need today, the Lord will provide it. Whatever you need tomorrow, the Lord will provide it. And you are free to eat of all the good things He offers to you, and called to trust that, if He has said "no," that is also His providence, that is also His way of caring for you. Trust. The Lord God will provide for all your needs, not when and how you think He should, but when and how is truly best for you.

Questions for reflection:

1. *When have you experienced the Lord providing for your needs, whether spiritual, emotional, or physical? How did He provide?*

2. *What has the Lord prohibited in your life that, looking back, you can see was for your good?*

3. *How is the Lord inviting you today to trust in His promise to provide for you? What do you need to surrender in order to trust more fully in Him?*

Action: In your spiritual journal, write down all the needs you are aware of in your life right now, and then make an act of faith for each one, repeating, "The Lord will provide," until you believe it. Then write "The Lord will provide" beside each of those needs.

THURSDAY, DECEMBER 5

"Everyone who listens to these words of mine and acts on them will be like a wise man who built his house on rock."

A reading from the Book of the Prophet Isaiah (26:1-6)

On that day they will sing this song in the land of Judah:
"A strong city have we;
he sets up walls and ramparts to protect us.
Open up the gates
to let in a nation that is just,
one that keeps faith.
A nation of firm purpose you keep in peace;
in peace, for its trust in you."

Trust in the LORD forever!
For the LORD is an eternal Rock.
He humbles those in high places,
and the lofty city he brings down;
He tumbles it to the ground,
levels it with the dust.
It is trampled underfoot by the needy,
by the footsteps of the poor.

Responsorial Psalm (118:1 and 8-9, 19-21, 25-27a)

R. **Blessed is he who comes in the name of the Lord.**
or:
R. **Alleluia**
Give thanks to the LORD, for he is good,
for his mercy endures forever.
It is better to take refuge in the LORD
than to trust in man.
It is better to take refuge in the LORD
than to trust in princes. R.

Open to me the gates of justice;
I will enter them and give thanks to the LORD.
This gate is the LORD's;
the just shall enter it.
I will give thanks to you, for you have answered me
and have been my savior. R.

O LORD, grant salvation!
O LORD, grant prosperity!
Blessed is he who comes in the name of the LORD;
we bless you from the house of the LORD.
The LORD is God, and he has given us light. R.

A reading from the holy Gospel according to Matthew
(7:21, 24-27)

Jesus said to his disciples:
"Not everyone who says to me, 'Lord, Lord,'
will enter the Kingdom of heaven,
but only the one who does the will of my Father in
    heaven.

"Everyone who listens to these words of mine and
    acts on them
will be like a wise man who built his house on rock.
The rain fell, the floods came,
and the winds blew and buffeted the house.
But it did not collapse; it had been set solidly on rock.
And everyone who listens to these words of mine
but does not act on them
will be like a fool who built his house on sand.
The rain fell, the floods came,
and the winds blew and buffeted the house.
And it collapsed and was completely ruined."

A few decades ago, a developer on the West Coast built an entire neighborhood of luxury homes, worth millions of dollars each, atop a sandstone cliff along the Oregon Coast. The homes were quickly sold. But within ten years, each of the homes in that development was condemned, as the sandstone cliff below them had been eroded by the ocean waves, and the homes were in danger of falling into the Pacific Ocean.

That's what Jesus is saying here. Building our lives on anything other than what He says—the One who created us, the one who knows our purpose and our destiny and exactly what will bring us there—is utter foolishness, a total waste, like the houses built on sandstone.

So often, we build our lives on such shaky ground, such shifting sands, such eroded cliffs. We might build on the wounds in our hearts, listening to so many lies about our identity and worth. We might build on what others think about us. We might build on our accomplishments or achievements, on our physical or mental capabilities. But all those things can change, can be washed away with the next storm, leaving our lives precariously in the balance.

There is only One who can tell us who we are and where and how to build our lives, because there is only One who created us. It's worthwhile always to remember this, to return to this: I am created, so I have a Creator. My Creator knows me. He's the One who spoke me into existence. What He says about my purpose, what He says about my identity, what He says about how to live— that is the only firm foundation for my life.

And what does He say? He says that I am worth more than the birds of the sky. He says that I am created out of love for love. He says that I have a mission and a purpose in life. He says that I am written on the palm of His hand. He says that His love for me will never be shaken. He says that, if I trust in Him, no harm will come to me.

So I can build my life on His word, the only firm foundation, the only solid rock. And then I can stand firm.

Questions for reflection:

1. *On what do you tend to base your sense of identity and self-worth? What does the Lord tell you today about that foundation?*

2. *What word of the Lord do you resist and why? (Perhaps a moral teaching, or a statement about your worth or goodness, etc.)*

3. *When have you experienced the security of building some aspect of your life on the foundation of God's Word?*

Action: Take a small stone and write on it a verse from Scripture that speaks to you about your identity as God's beloved creature.

"The lowly shall ever find joy in the Lord."

A reading from the Book of the Prophet Isaiah (29:17-24)

Thus says the Lord GOD:
But a very little while,
and Lebanon shall be changed into an orchard,
and the orchard be regarded as a forest!
On that day the deaf shall hear
the words of a book;
And out of gloom and darkness,
the eyes of the blind shall see.
The lowly will ever find joy in the LORD,
and the poor rejoice in the Holy One of Israel.
For the tyrant will be no more
and the arrogant will have gone;
All who are alert to do evil will be cut off,
those whose mere word condemns a man,
Who ensnare his defender at the gate,
and leave the just man with an empty claim.
Therefore thus says the LORD,
the God of the house of Jacob,
who redeemed Abraham:
Now Jacob shall have nothing to be ashamed of,
nor shall his face grow pale.
When his children see
the work of my hands in his midst,
They shall keep my name holy;
they shall reverence the Holy One of Jacob,
and be in awe of the God of Israel.
Those who err in spirit shall acquire understanding,
and those who find fault shall receive instruction.

R. **The Lord is my light and my salvation.**

The LORD is my light and my salvation;
whom should I fear?
The LORD is my life's refuge;
 of whom should I be afraid? R.

One thing I ask of the LORD;
this I seek:
To dwell in the house of the LORD
all the days of my life,
That I may gaze on the loveliness of the LORD
and contemplate his temple. R.

I believe that I shall see the bounty of the LORD
in the land of the living.
Wait for the LORD with courage;
be stouthearted, and wait for the LORD. R.

A reading from the holy Gospel according to Matthew
(9:27-31)

As Jesus passed by, two blind men followed him,
    crying out,
"Son of David, have pity on us!"
When he entered the house,
the blind men approached him and Jesus said to them,
"Do you believe that I can do this?"
"Yes, Lord," they said to him.
Then he touched their eyes and said,
"Let it be done for you according to your faith."
And their eyes were opened.
Jesus warned them sternly,
"See that no one knows about this."
But they went out and spread word of him through all
    that land.

In Dante's *Purgatorio*, at the first level of the seven-story mountain of Purgatory, the penance of the prideful is to walk stooped low to the ground, carrying a heavy weight. Because they lifted themselves up too high for their own good during their lifetime, because they were prideful and took any gifts they had as coming from themselves, now they are being brought back to the reality of who they are, in preparation for heaven. They are remembering that they are merely human creatures. Even at the root of the word "human" is the word *humus*, the Latin word for "dust" or "ground." It's related, of course, to the word "humiliation," which brings us back down when we raise ourselves up, and to the virtue of "humility," which is to walk in the truth of our created humanity, of our being made from the dust.

Genesis tells us that God formed Adam from the dust of the earth and breathed into Adam the breath of life; that's how man became a living being. We can never forget we are dust and to dust we shall return, as we are reminded each year on Ash Wednesday. Why?

Because when we forget that we are dust, we begin to live with a sense of entitlement. When we live with a sense of entitlement, we lose sight of the beautiful fact that everything we have, including our own existence, is a gift that we did nothing to merit. We forget that we exist because the Creator of the universe has gifted us with life and with every talent and every capability we have.

It's worth pondering again and again, going back day after day to the many gifts we receive each day, starting with the basic fact that, if we are reading this, we are alive. And for every challenge or difficulty, for every wound or suffering in our lives, there are always far more blessings. Can you breathe? Did you do anything to earn that ability? Can you think? Can you move, see, hear, speak, smell, taste?

There are millions of unnoticed gifts in our lives each day; when we stop to ponder them, to recognize them, we are in a sense eating of all the good fruits of the garden again, all the gifts that the Lord has for us. There is no need to focus on what I don't have, what is lacking, what I wish were different, because God is showering down gifts on me that I have never even stopped to notice.

It's the lowly who notice the good things. It's the lowly who recognize that everything is a gift. It's the lowly who can live in poverty with joyful hearts. It's the lowly who can share in the Virgin Mary's hymn of praise to the Lord, joyful because He has looked with favor on their poverty and chosen to bless them.

So today, let's live with lowly hearts. Let's let go of all the things we feel entitled to, whether from God, from life, or from others. Let's instead keep our hearts open to perceive and receive all the many good gifts the Father is giving us today, so we can savor them, so we can recognize that there is nothing that we lack.

Questions for reflection:

1. *What good things in your life do you tend to take for granted? What changes about your attitude toward them when you begin to thank the Father for them?*

2. *In what ways do you tend to focus on what is missing or what you wish were different? Where does the Lord invite you to turn your attention today?*

3. *How have you experienced the connection between humility and joy?*

Action: Spend at least five minutes today simply thanking God for every gift you've received in this day, beginning with the fact that you are alive.

SATURDAY, DECEMBER 7
*"A voice shall sound in your ears:
'This is the way; walk in it.'"*

A reading from the Book of the Prophet Isaiah
(30:19-21, 23-26)

Thus says the Lord GOD,
the Holy One of Israel:
O people of Zion, who dwell in Jerusalem,
no more will you weep;
He will be gracious to you when you cry out,
as soon as he hears he will answer you.
The Lord will give you the bread you need
and the water for which you thirst.
No longer will your Teacher hide himself,
but with your own eyes you shall see your Teacher,
While from behind, a voice shall sound in your ears:
"This is the way; walk in it,"
when you would turn to the right or to the left.

He will give rain for the seed
that you sow in the ground,
And the wheat that the soil produces
will be rich and abundant.
On that day your flock will be given pasture
and the lamb will graze in spacious meadows;
The oxen and the asses that till the ground
will eat silage tossed to them
with shovel and pitchfork.
Upon every high mountain and lofty hill
there will be streams of running water.
On the day of the great slaughter,
when the towers fall,

The light of the moon will be like that of the sun
and the light of the sun will be seven times greater
like the light of seven days.
On the day the LORD binds up the wounds of his
    people,
he will heal the bruises left by his blows.

R. **Blessed are all who wait for the Lord.**

Praise the LORD, for he is good;
sing praise to our God, for he is gracious;
it is fitting to praise him.
The LORD rebuilds Jerusalem;
the dispersed of Israel he gathers. R.

He heals the brokenhearted
and binds up their wounds.
He tells the number of the stars;
he calls each by name. R.

Great is our LORD and mighty in power:
to his wisdom there is no limit.
The LORD sustains the lowly;
the wicked he casts to the ground. R.

A reading from the holy Gospel according to Matthew
(9:35–10:1, 5a, 6-8)

Jesus went around to all the towns and villages,
teaching in their synagogues,
proclaiming the Gospel of the Kingdom,
and curing every disease and illness.
At the sight of the crowds, his heart was moved with
    pity for them

because they were troubled and abandoned,
like sheep without a shepherd.
Then he said to his disciples,
"The harvest is abundant but the laborers are few;
so ask the master of the harvest
to send out laborers for his harvest."

Then he summoned his Twelve disciples
and gave them authority over unclean spirits to drive them out
and to cure every disease and every illness.

Jesus sent out these Twelve after instructing them thus,
"Go to the lost sheep of the house of Israel.
As you go, make this proclamation: 'The Kingdom of heaven is at hand.'
Cure the sick, raise the dead,
cleanse lepers, drive out demons.
Without cost you have received; without cost you are to give."

Some years back, I was teaching First Communion preparation to a group of troubled children in another country. Many of those kids had been expelled from the private school where we taught First Communion, an after-school option, but the school allowed them back for sacramental prep. It was a tough assignment, still not having mastered the language, with a group of nine-year-olds, some of whom seemed like fighting or ripping things off of bulletin boards were their preferred activities.

But when it was time to teach on conscience, my co-teacher and I received a light from the Holy Spirit. We asked them, "When you do something bad, what do you feel?" "Bad," they unanimously responded. One little boy, Peter, added, "Miss, it's because we're bad. That's why we do bad things."

But we disagreed. "Peter, if you really were bad, when you do bad things, you would feel *good* about what you've just done."

"But we don't feel good," they responded. "Every time we do something bad, we feel bad."

"Well, that's proof that you're *good*. That you are not meant to do bad things. That feeling inside, that voice that says you've done something wrong, that's your conscience. And what it's telling you is that you're good, and that you're made to do good things."

One of the gifts God gave us in creation, a gift that we still have, is our conscience. The Catechism says that when a person listens to his fully formed conscience, he hears God speaking to him. Conscience is the internal voice of God's law, given to us to help us discern right from wrong. *Gaudium et Spes* puts it this way: "In the depths of his conscience, man detects a law which he does not impose upon himself, but which holds him to obedience. Always summoning him to love good and avoid evil, the voice of conscience when necessary speaks to his heart: do this, shun that....to obey it is the very dignity of man."

In our conscience, the Church teaches us, we are alone with God, and we can choose freely to follow the voice of our conscience, choose freely to follow the voice of God. Conscience is proof that we were created *good* and that even as we are now, we are not evil. It is the voice of God speaking within us, pointing out the right path.

Of course, we have to let the Lord form our conscience, through His Word, through the teachings of the Church, and through our own right choices—which is what my students learned that day. Because they really *are* good, they could choose to *do* good. And so can we. And so must we, if we are going to become all that God created us to be.

Questions for reflection:

1. *Call to mind a time when you did something contrary to your conscience: what did you experience? Why did you choose to go against your conscience? What were the results?*

2. *Call to mind a time when you acted according to your conscience. What did you experience? What were the results?*

3. *In what ways has your conscience been de-formed, either by things you have learned or things you have done? What step can you take today to begin to re-form it?*

Action: Draw a one-way street sign, and write on it, "This is the way." Place it over or next to something that for you is a source of temptation.

WEEK TWO

CAPTURED

This second week of Advent, we meditate on the second part of the *kerygma*, the bad news, that we have been captured by the Enemy, that we are under the powers of sin and death. That is to say, we meditate on the Fall and the consequences of the Fall, not just for Adam and Eve but for all of humanity, for you and for me. As we enter into this week, let's ask the Lord for courage: to face this reality, to face our own brokenness and sinfulness, and to be convicted of our need for a Rescuer.

If done well, the meditations this week should prepare you for a good confession, a necessary step for experiencing the rescue that Jesus came to bring, and for preparing our hearts for Christmas. So don't skip writing down your answers to the questions, as that will be the basis for a good confession.

"He went throughout the whole region of the Jordan, proclaiming baptism of repentance for the forgiveness of sins."

A reading from the Book of the Prophet Baruch (5:1-9)

Jerusalem, take off your robe of mourning and misery;
  put on the splendor of glory from God forever:
wrapped in the cloak of justice from God,
    bear on your head the mitre
    that displays the glory of the eternal name.
For God will show all the earth your splendor:
    you will be named by God forever
    the peace of justice, the glory of God's worship.

Up, Jerusalem! stand upon the heights;
    look to the east and see your children
gathered from the east and the west
    at the word of the Holy One,
    rejoicing that they are remembered by God.
Led away on foot by their enemies they left you:
    but God will bring them back to you
    borne aloft in glory as on royal thrones.
For God has commanded
    that every lofty mountain be made low,
and that the age-old depths and gorges
    be filled to level ground,
    that Israel may advance secure in the glory of God.
The forests and every fragrant kind of tree
    have overshadowed Israel at God's command;
for God is leading Israel in joy
    by the light of his glory,
    with his mercy and justice for company.

R. **The Lord has done great things for us; we are filled with joy.**

When the LORD brought back the captives of Zion,
  we were like men dreaming.
Then our mouth was filled with laughter,
  and our tongue with rejoicing. R.

Then they said among the nations,
  "The LORD has done great things for them."
The LORD has done great things for us;
  we are glad indeed. R.

Restore our fortunes, O LORD,
  like the torrents in the southern desert.
Those who sow in tears
  shall reap rejoicing. R.

Although they go forth weeping,
  carrying the seed to be sown,
They shall come back rejoicing,
  carrying their sheaves. R.

A reading from the Letter of St. Paul to the Phillipians
(1:4-6, 8-11)

Brothers and sisters:
I pray always with joy in my every prayer for all of you,
because of your partnership for the gospel
from the first day until now.
I am confident of this,
that the one who began a good work in you
will continue to complete it
until the day of Christ Jesus.
God is my witness,

how I long for all of you with the affection of Christ
Jesus.
And this is my prayer:
that your love may increase ever more and more
in knowledge and every kind of perception,
to discern what is of value,
so that you may be pure and blameless for the day of
Christ,
filled with the fruit of righteousness
that comes through Jesus Christ
for the glory and praise of God.

A reading from the holy Gospel according to Luke (3:1-6)

In the fifteenth year of the reign of Tiberius Caesar,
when Pontius Pilate was governor of Judea,
and Herod was tetrarch of Galilee,
and his brother Philip tetrarch of the region
of Ituraea and Trachonitis,
and Lysanias was tetrarch of Abilene,
during the high priesthood of Annas and Caiaphas,
the word of God came to John the son of Zechariah
in the desert.
John went throughout the whole region of the
Jordan,
proclaiming a baptism of repentance for the
forgiveness of sins,
as it is written in the book of the words of the
prophet Isaiah:
A voice of one crying out in the desert:
"Prepare the way of the Lord,
make straight his paths.
Every valley shall be filled
and every mountain and hill shall be made low.

The winding roads shall be made straight,
and the rough ways made smooth,
and all flesh shall see the salvation of God."

Repentance. It's not a very common word in our current cultural climate. When famous people feel forced to make a public recognition for their wrongdoing, they will say something like, "I deeply regret," or "I'm very sorry." But almost never do you hear someone say, "I repent with my whole heart."

There's a big difference between feeling sorry and repenting, between regretting and repenting. Regret is feeling bad about something one has done. Repentance means to change one's direction, to change one's thinking, to turn from the wrongdoing and turn back to God. Repentance means to see sin for what it is, to see it in all of its ugliness, and to own up to it, to recognize that I have done that, to turn away from it, and to ask the One who created me to set me free from it.

In our ministry to the homeless, the majority of our friendships are with people who are addicted to substances. Over and over, we will hear of their regret for the addiction, even of a desire to change, to get clean. But repentance? It's not so common, and it's not so easy.

Repentance is something we can't come to on our own. Regret, yeah, we can muster that. Being sorry, yep, that's within our reach. Even apologizing is something under our control. But repentance, true repentance, requires the grace of God. It requires Someone greater than I, Someone freer than I, to come and pull me out of whatever trap I've stepped into by sinning.

Until we've repented, we can't receive forgiveness. Yes, God has already forgiven us on Calvary, Jesus taking upon Himself all of our sins. Forgiveness has been granted to us. But if we are still holding on to our sin, contenting ourselves with feeling regret or remorse, we can't receive that forgiveness, because rather than turning to the One who offers it to us, we are still turned toward our sin.

So let's ask Jesus in this week to come and to rescue us. Whatever sin we feel bad about but are not ready to fully turn from, let's ask Him to give us the grace of true repentance. And let's do all we can to cooperate with that grace—to turn, step by step if necessary, from sin and toward Him.

Questions for reflection:

1. *What things in your life have you regretted doing but have not yet repented of? What will it take to bring you to repentance?*

2. *When have you experienced the power of Jesus rescuing you through the grace of repentance? What were the fruits of that repentance in your life?*

3. *When have you truly known God's forgiveness in your life? What step can you take today to know that forgiveness in a new way?*

Action: Write in big block letters the word REPENT on a sticky note, and stick it over something that is a source of continued temptation for you.

Again, what is offered below is a suggestion for how a priest or deacon may choose to preach the kerygma this week based on *The Rescue Project*. Last week we looked at the question "Why is there something rather than nothing?" and the word Created. This week we focus on the question "Why is everything so obviously messed up?" and the word Captured.

2nd Sunday of Advent
Part Two: Captured

Ask God for the grace of "despair" (Meaning, the grace to understand how utterly hopeless we were before God's Son came to rescue us.)

Key Themes: Again, any of these are worth exploring this week. The key is to ask the Lord what is most significant for your particular community!

- Scripture is like "game film." It equips us with the tactics of the opponent, the one and only enemy of the human race. It reveals not simply "what happened" but "what always happens."

- There is only one God. Satan is not a rival to God; he is a creature.

- Satan was created good by God. He was an angel. His sin is pride but his motive for rebelling against God is envy (cf. Wisdom 2:24).

- He has declared war on the creature God loves the most: the human race. He hates us.

- His root strategy is to tempt us to think that either God is not a good Father and cannot be trusted, or that we could be happier apart from God.

- His tactics include: lies, accusations, division, flattery, discouragement, and temptations.

- His goal is simple: our personal destruction.

- When our first parents fell for his deception, they unknowingly sold our race into slavery to powers we can never defeat on our own: Sin and Death, both of which Scripture speaks of not only as events that will happen to us (Death), or things that we do or don't do (Sin), but as governments and authorities.

- The "grace" of despair can help us understand how utterly hopeless our situation is. We have been captured, there is no way out on our own, and we need someone to rescue us from these powers.

Questions for Reflection:

- Do I believe there is an enemy who has a plan to ruin my life?

- How do I see Satan and the demons after contemplating all of this?

- What lies and accusations is the enemy tempting me with *right now*?

Possible Verses for Focus from Today's Readings:

Baruch (5:1): "Take off your robe of mourning and misery."

[The ultimate cause of this mourning and misery is the hopeless situation the human race finds itself in: slavery to Sin, Death, and Satan.]

Psalms (126): "When the LORD brought back the captives of Zion, / we were like men dreaming. / Then our mouth was filled with laughter, / and our tongue with rejoicing."

[The captivity the Israelites were experiencing was real, and yet also an image of the real captivity the human race finds itself in: to Sin and Death. Yet see what God does: He brings His creation out of that captivity!]

Philippians (1:6): "the one who began a good work in you will continue to complete it until the day of Christ Jesus."

[God has done something about our slavery. He has defeated Sin, Death, and Satan already by His cross and resurrection. However, He has not yet destroyed them. That will only happen when the Lord returns in glory (i.e. "the day of Christ Jesus.")]

Luke (3:3): "John went throughout the whole region of the Jordan, proclaiming a baptism of repentance for the forgiveness of sins."

[While it's true that we are enslaved to Sin and Death, we also have to accept responsibility for the fact that we often connive in our own slavery. We are not innocent victims, but often willing cooperators with evil and therefore need to acknowledge that and ask for forgiveness.]

Luke (3:6): "all flesh shall see the salvation of God."

[Salvation could also be translated as "rescue" or "deliverance." This begs the question, Salvation, rescue and deliverance from what? From whom? From Death, from Sin, from Satan. God is faithful; He acts; He rescues; He loves!]

NOTES

NOTES

MONDAY, DECEMBER 9,
FEAST OF THE IMMACULATE CONCEPTION
OF THE BLESSED VIRGIN MARY

"He chose us in him before the foundation of the world,
to be holy and without blemish before him."

A reading from the Book of Genesis (3:9-15, 20)

After the man, Adam, had eaten of the tree,
the LORD God called to the man and asked him,
   "Where are you?"
He answered, "I heard you in the garden;
but I was afraid, because I was naked,
so I hid myself."
Then he asked, "Who told you that you were naked?
You have eaten, then,
from the tree of which I had forbidden you to eat!"
The man replied, "The woman whom you put here
   with me—
she gave me fruit from the tree, and so I ate it."
The LORD God then asked the woman,
"Why did you do such a thing?"
The woman answered, "The serpent tricked me into
   it, so I ate it."

Then the LORD God said to the serpent:
"Because you have done this, you shall be banned
from all the animals
and from all the wild creatures;
on your belly shall you crawl,
and dirt shall you eat
all the days of your life.
I will put enmity between you and the woman,
and between your offspring and hers;

he will strike at your head,
while you strike at his heel."

The man called his wife Eve,
because she became the mother of all the living.

R. **Sing to the Lord a new song, for he has done mar-
velous deeds.**

Sing to the LORD a new song,
for he has done wondrous deeds;
His right hand has won victory for him,
his holy arm. R.

The LORD has made his salvation known:
in the sight of the nations he has revealed his justice.
He has remembered his kindness and his faithfulness
toward the house of Israel. R.

All the ends of the earth have seen
the salvation by our God.
Sing joyfully to the LORD, all you lands;
break into song; sing praise. R.

A reading from the Letter of St. Paul to the Ephesians
(1:3-6, 11-12)

Brothers and sisters:
Blessed be the God and Father of our Lord Jesus
    Christ,
who has blessed us in Christ
with every spiritual blessing in the heavens,
as he chose us in him, before the foundation of the
    world,
to be holy and without blemish before him.

In love he destined us for adoption to himself through
   Jesus Christ,
in accord with the favor of his will,
for the praise of the glory of his grace
that he granted us in the beloved.

In him we were also chosen,
destined in accord with the purpose of the One
who accomplishes all things according to the
   intention of his will,
so that we might exist for the praise of his glory,
we who first hoped in Christ.

A reading from the holy Gospel according to Luke
(1:26-38)

The angel Gabriel was sent from God
to a town of Galilee called Nazareth,
to a virgin betrothed to a man named Joseph,
of the house of David,
and the virgin's name was Mary.
And coming to her, he said,
"Hail, full of grace! The Lord is with you."
But she was greatly troubled at what was said
and pondered what sort of greeting this might be.
Then the angel said to her,
"Do not be afraid, Mary,
for you have found favor with God.
Behold, you will conceive in your womb and bear a son,
and you shall name him Jesus.
He will be great and will be called Son of the Most High,
and the Lord God will give him the throne of David his
   father,
and he will rule over the house of Jacob forever,
and of his Kingdom there will be no end."

But Mary said to the angel,
"How can this be,
since I have no relations with a man?"
And the angel said to her in reply,
"The Holy Spirit will come upon you,
and the power of the Most High will overshadow you.
Therefore the child to be born
will be called holy, the Son of God.
And behold, Elizabeth, your relative,
has also conceived a son in her old age,
and this is the sixth month for her who was called
    barren;
for nothing will be impossible for God."
Mary said, "Behold, I am the handmaid of the Lord.
May it be done to me according to your word."
Then the angel departed from her.

How were we created to be? The Lord, in His great goodness, has left us a perfect example, a clear and untarnished image of humanity as He created it. Her name is Mary, and when we look at her, we see who He created us to be from the beginning. We see the unsullied, perfect, grace-filled nature of our first parents and the image of our re-creation. So it's worthwhile, on this special day, to spend some time contemplating Mary, because when we look at her, we see who we are created to be—and who, with His grace, we will become.

The first thing we learn in Scripture about Mary's character is told us in the greeting of the angel Gabriel: "Hail, full of grace!" Full of grace—when a vessel is full of something, there is no room in it for anything else. If a glass is filled to the brim with water, there's no space left for coffee or milk. The angel names her "full of grace," which is to say that her whole soul, her whole being, is a pure vessel, that the only thing in her is grace, which means there's no room for disorder, for sin, for selfishness of any sort, for unbelief, or for anything else that is contrary to God's grace.

The next thing we learn is that she ponders the words that come to her from God, the message of the angel. His words trouble her, but she doesn't reject them or flee from them; instead, she holds them in her heart and mind, weighing them, seeking to understand them. She reflects on God's word, lets it change her and move her to action.

And then we see that she asks a question of the angel, a question not in order to defend herself or change God's plan, but a question in order to understand what it is that is being asked of her, how she can cooperate with God's plan. She enters into dialogue with God.

And when she understands more fully, but without still fully understanding (how could she know what it means that she will become pregnant because "the power of the Most High will overshadow" her?), her response is a simple, trusting surrender, an act of loving obedience: "Behold, I am the handmaid of the Lord. May it be done to me according to your word."

This is our calling, too. This was how Adam and Eve were created, too—to be filled with God's grace, to ponder the words that come from God and hold onto them, to enter into dialogue with Him when they didn't fully understand His messages, and always, in all things, to trust and surrender, knowing that He is Lord and we are mere creatures. We are neither in the state of Adam and Eve nor in the state of the Virgin Mary. But we can model our lives off of hers, surrendering, like her, in trusting obedience to every word that comes forth from the mouth of God.

Questions for reflection:

1. *In what ways in this past year have you heard the Lord speak to you? How have you responded to His messages?*

2. *How quickly do you tend to respond to the Lord? What are your usual resistances?*

3. *When have you surrendered to the Lord? What has been the result?*

Action: Write the word "FIAT" on something you will see throughout the day, and make that your response to the Lord for each thing He asks of you today.

A reading from the Book of the Prophet Isaiah (40:1-11)

Comfort, give comfort to my people,
says your God.
Speak tenderly to Jerusalem, and proclaim to her
that her service is at an end,
her guilt is expiated;
Indeed, she has received from the hand of the LORD
double for all her sins.

A voice cries out:
In the desert prepare the way of the LORD!
Make straight in the wasteland a highway for our God!
Every valley shall be filled in,
every mountain and hill shall be made low;
The rugged land shall be made a plain,
the rough country, a broad valley.
Then the glory of the LORD shall be revealed,
and all people shall see it together;
for the mouth of the LORD has spoken.

A voice says, "Cry out!"
I answer, "What shall I cry out?"
"All flesh is grass,
and all their glory like the flower of the field.
The grass withers, the flower wilts,
when the breath of the LORD blows upon it.
So then, the people is the grass.
Though the grass withers and the flower wilts,
the word of our God stands forever."

Go up onto a high mountain,
Zion, herald of glad tidings;
Cry out at the top of your voice,
Jerusalem, herald of good news!
Fear not to cry out
and say to the cities of Judah:
Here is your God!
Here comes with power
the Lord GOD,
who rules by his strong arm;
Here is his reward with him,
his recompense before him.
Like a shepherd he feeds his flock;
in his arms he gathers the lambs,
Carrying them in his bosom,
and leading the ewes with care.

Responsorial Psalm (96:1-2, 3 and 10ac, 11-12, 13)

R. **The Lord our God comes with power.**

Sing to the LORD a new song;
sing to the LORD, all you lands.
Sing to the LORD; bless his name;
announce his salvation, day after day. R.

Tell his glory among the nations;
among all peoples, his wondrous deeds.
Say among the nations: The LORD is king;
he governs the peoples with equity. R.

Let the heavens be glad and the earth rejoice;
let the sea and what fills it resound;
let the plains be joyful and all that is in them!
Then let all the trees of the forest rejoice. R.

They shall exult before the LORD, for he comes;
for he comes to rule the earth.
He shall rule the world with justice
and the peoples with his constancy. R.

A reading from the holy Gospel according to Matthew
(18:12-14)

Jesus said to his disciples:
"What is your opinion?
If a man has a hundred sheep and one of them goes
astray,
will he not leave the ninety-nine in the hills
and go in search of the stray?
And if he finds it, amen, I say to you, he rejoices more
over it
than over the ninety-nine that did not stray.
In just the same way, it is not the will of your heavenly
Father
that one of these little ones be lost."

Ever since I was a little child, this short parable has moved me profoundly, because of the vividness of the imagery I see in my mind. Picture it with me, if you will.

All the flock is roaming around the fields, the little lambs frolicking, jumping, running, generally close to their mothers, close to the flock. But one little lamb wanders off by himself, exploring the edge of the meadow. Caught up in this new adventure, he neglects to follow the flock when it moves, and just keeps exploring.

Soon, he has gone off the pasture, and without him even feeling it, because of his wool he starts to get caught by brambles, and before he realizes what is happening he finds himself entangled, unable to move freely. The harder he tries to free himself, the deeper the brambles dig in, until some are past the wool, actually touching his skin. He begins to bleat and cry out, but separated from the flock, he is unheard. He is trapped, sad, and alone. And now the sun is going down, and darkness is setting in, and at a distance, he hears a coyote howl. He trembles in fear.

Whatever he tries, he cannot free himself. He is stuck. He needs a rescuer.

And a rescuer comes. The shepherd leaves the 99 safe in the fold, and comes to the lost lamb, breaking away the brambles, lifting up the dirty, tired, trembling lamb, and placing him over his shoulders.

"It's okay," he says, "It's okay. I'm here. You're safe. We're going home. You don't have to stay here. You're not stuck anymore, you're not trapped anymore, you're not alone anymore. You're free. You're safe. We're going home."

Wherever you are stuck today, Jesus is coming for you. Whatever mess you've gotten yourself into, you're not doomed to stay in it—Jesus is coming to break you free. It doesn't matter that you did it to yourself, that you wandered away on your own, that you chose to be here in the first place. What matters is that your Rescuer is on the way, and He will break you free, will bring you home. So don't let the Enemy discourage you. Yes, he is a roaring lion seeking to devour you. But he is no match for your Shepherd.

Questions for reflection:

1. *In what ways do I tend to wander off on my own, away from the safety of the faith community? Why do I do this?*

2. *How has sin isolated me from others? What steps do I need to take to return to community?*

3. *Where do you need Jesus to come in and rescue you today?*

Action: Listen to or sing the song "The King of Love My Shepherd Is" today.

A reading from the Book of the Prophet Isaiah
(40:25-31)

To whom can you liken me as an equal?
says the Holy One.
Lift up your eyes on high
and see who has created these things:
He leads out their army and numbers them,
calling them all by name.
By his great might and the strength of his power
not one of them is missing!
Why, O Jacob, do you say,
and declare, O Israel,
"My way is hidden from the LORD,
and my right is disregarded by my God"?

Do you not know
or have you not heard?
The LORD is the eternal God,
creator of the ends of the earth.
He does not faint nor grow weary,
and his knowledge is beyond scrutiny.
He gives strength to the fainting;
for the weak he makes vigor abound.
Though young men faint and grow weary,
and youths stagger and fall,
They that hope in the LORD will renew their strength,
they will soar as with eagles' wings;
They will run and not grow weary,
walk and not grow faint.

R. **O bless the Lord, my soul!**

Bless the LORD, O my soul;
and all my being, bless his holy name.
Bless the LORD, O my soul,
and forget not all his benefits. R.

He pardons all your iniquities,
he heals all your ills.
He redeems your life from destruction,
he crowns you with kindness and compassion. R.

Merciful and gracious is the LORD,
slow to anger and abounding in kindness.
Not according to our sins does he deal with us,
nor does he requite us according to our crimes. R.

A reading from the holy Gospel according to Matthew
(11:28-30)

Jesus said to the crowds:
"Come to me, all you who labor and are burdened,
and I will give you rest.
Take my yoke upon you and learn from me,
for I am meek and humble of heart;
and you will find rest for yourselves.
For my yoke is easy, and my burden light."

Back at the time of the Revolutionary War, Patrick Henry famously cried out in a speech to the Second Virginia Convention, "Give me liberty or give me death!" And somehow that sentiment has entered into our bone marrow in the United States. Give me liberty or give me death. I don't want to be controlled by anyone, by anything.

So this teaching of Jesus, "Take my yoke upon you and learn from me," is hard for us to accept. We would rather Jesus said something like, "Here's a GPS device—go where you want, when you want, how you want." But that's not what He says. He says, "take my yoke upon you," and we instinctively resist that image. It seems so *limiting*. How can I be free if I am *yoked* to someone else?

One of the things the Enemy did when he deceived our first parents was to convince them that the only real freedom is freedom *from* any kind of constraint. "You will be like gods," he tells them. That is, you will be able to determine for yourself what is right and wrong—no one can tell you what to do.

And we fell for it. We swallowed the whole lie and all of its consequences, and so find ourselves enslaved by this very ideal of freedom, of absolute liberty.

But freedom, true freedom, isn't really freedom from any constraint on my action—because, metaphysically and physically, it is impossible to have no constraints, no limits. I am this body that I am, not some other body. I am bound to this planet by the law of gravity. I am not all-knowing or all-powerful. I am not, and never will be, God, no matter how much the false promise of absolute freedom insists that I am or can be.

The only true freedom is the freedom to do what is good and right and just with ease, the freedom that comes from being yoked to Jesus Christ. Because if I am not yoked to Jesus, I am yoked to the Enemy.

The freedom that Jesus promises is real freedom, freedom to choose the good, freedom to strengthen our will, freedom to become who we were created to be, the glorious freedom of the children of God.

The freedom that the Enemy promises is illusory, binding us to sin, deepening the pit in which we've fallen.

Either we choose the yoke of Christ, or we choose the chains of sin. We have no other option.

Questions for reflection:

1. *In what areas of my life do I tend to fall into the ideal of freedom from any kind of limit or constraint? What are the consequences when I follow this ideal?*

2. *In what ways has yoking myself to Christ brought about greater freedom in my life so far?*

3. *What is the choice set before me today? What does the Enemy promise? What does Christ promise?*

Action: Draw or print an image of a wooden yoke and write on it: "Freedom."

THURSDAY, DECEMBER 12,
FEAST OF OUR LADY OF GUADALUPE

"It was a huge dragon...
its tail swept away a third of the stars in the sky."

A reading from the Book of the Prophet Zechariah
(2:14-17)

Sing and rejoice, O daughter Zion!
See, I am coming to dwell among you, says the
 LORD.
Many nations shall join themselves to the LORD on
 that day,
and they shall be his people,
and he will dwell among you,
and you shall know that the LORD of hosts has
 sent me to you.
The LORD will possess Judah as his portion in the
 holy land,
and he will again choose Jerusalem.
Silence, all mankind, in the presence of the LORD!
For he stirs forth from his holy dwelling.

or

A reading from the Book of Revelation
(11:19a; 12:1-6a, 10ab)

God's temple in heaven was opened,
and the ark of his covenant could be seen in the temple.

A great sign appeared in the sky, a woman clothed
 with the sun,
with the moon under her feet,
and on her head a crown of twelve stars.

She was with child and wailed aloud in pain as she
    labored to give birth.
Then another sign appeared in the sky;
it was a huge red dragon, with seven heads and ten
    horns,
and on its heads were seven diadems.
Its tail swept away a third of the stars in the sky
and hurled them down to the earth.
Then the dragon stood before the woman about to
    give birth,
to devour her child when she gave birth.
She gave birth to a son, a male child,
destined to rule all the nations with an iron rod.
Her child was caught up to God and his throne.
The woman herself fled into the desert
where she had a place prepared by God.

Then I heard a loud voice in heaven say:
"Now have salvation and power come,
and the Kingdom of our God
and the authority of his Anointed."

Responsorial Psalm (Judith 13:18BCDE, 19)

R. **You are the highest honor of our race.**

Blessed are you, daughter, by the Most High God,
above all the women on earth;
and blessed be the LORD God,
the creator of heaven and earth. R.

Your deed of hope will never be forgotten
by those who tell of the might of God. R.

The angel Gabriel was sent from God
to a town of Galilee called Nazareth,
to a virgin betrothed to a man named Joseph,
of the house of David,
and the virgin's name was Mary.
And coming to her, he said,
"Hail, full of grace! The Lord is with you."
But she was greatly troubled at what was said
and pondered what sort of greeting this might be.
Then the angel said to her,
"Do not be afraid, Mary,
for you have found favor with God.
Behold, you will conceive in your womb and bear a son,
and you shall name him Jesus.
He will be great and will be called Son of the Most High,
and the Lord God will give him the throne of David his
    father,
and he will rule over the house of Jacob forever,
and of his Kingdom there will be no end."
But Mary said to the angel,
"How can this be,
since I have no relations with a man?"
And the angel said to her in reply,
"The Holy Spirit will come upon you,
and the power of the Most High will overshadow you.
Therefore the child to be born
will be called holy, the Son of God.
And behold, Elizabeth, your relative,
has also conceived a son in her old age,
and this is the sixth month for her who was called barren;
for nothing will be impossible for God."

Mary said, "Behold, I am the handmaid of the Lord.
May it be done to me according to your word."
Then the angel departed from her.

or

A reading from the holy Gospel according to Luke
(1:39-47)

Mary set out
and traveled to the hill country in haste
to a town of Judah,
where she entered the house of Zechariah
and greeted Elizabeth.
When Elizabeth heard Mary's greeting,
the infant leaped in her womb,
and Elizabeth, filled with the Holy Spirit,
cried out in a loud voice and said,
"Most blessed are you among women,
and blessed is the fruit of your womb.
And how does this happen to me,
that the mother of my Lord should come to me?
For at the moment the sound of your greeting
    reached my ears,
the infant in my womb leaped for joy.
Blessed are you who believed
that what was spoken to you by the Lord
would be fulfilled."
And Mary said:

"My soul proclaims the greatness of the Lord;
my spirit rejoices in God my savior."

When Our Lady of Guadalupe first appeared to San Juan
Diego in Mexico in 1531, the people of Mexico were still
reeling from having suffered the brutality of Aztec rule for

more than 200 years—above all, the brutality of human sacrifices. Historians estimate that 50,000 people were sacrificed each year to the Aztec god Huitzilopochtli, the god of the sun, who required the blood of human hearts to keep the sun burning. As the priests cut out the beating hearts of their victims, they held the heart before the dying eyes of the human sacrifice, then hacked off the victim's arms and legs and threw them out to the crowd, who would take them home, cook them, and eat them.

What? How can it be that such cruelty and violence, such bloodthirst, could be instituted as the worship of a "god"? How could humans be so brutal toward one another?

It's inexplicable, really. Scientifically, it has nothing to do with the theory of the survival of the fittest, because that level of cruelty goes far beyond any need for survival. Anthropologically, there is little agreement about whether anything can be called evil. But what else can you call it?

In a thought experiment with my freshman students last fall, I asked them if they think everything in the world is as it should be. They adamantly insisted that it is not, from practicing Catholics to ardent atheists, all agreeing that human cruelty is not how we are supposed to be, that sickness and death, violence and war, go against something basic, something that should be but is not. While the atheists didn't have an explanation, they were insistent that somehow, in some way, things got very deeply messed up.

Scripture offers an explanation, and given all the other possibilities, given the 50,000 human sacrifices each year in Aztec Mexico, given the violence and wars, the child abuse, the disease, and so many other things that are so clearly wrong with the world, it's the only answer that really makes sense of the problem of evil. The answer is that we have an Enemy, a very powerful one (though still a creature), a fallen angel who hates the human race and wants to destroy us because he is envious of us. Scripture calls him Satan, the devil, the accuser, the deceiver, the serpent.

He hates us. He envies us. And all through our history, both the history of humanity and our own personal history, he has been trying to destroy us. He lies to us, tries to convince us that God is against us. He deceives us into sinning. He accuses God and he accuses others and he accuses us. He divides—if he can separate us from others, he has a better chance of defeating us. He tempts us. And when we have fallen for any of his tactics, he discourages us.

He is the Enemy of our souls. Any evil you have suffered in your life, Satan was ultimately behind it, trying to destroy you.

But he doesn't get the last word. When Our Lady appeared in 1531 to St. Juan Diego, she appeared standing in front of the sun, greater than Huitzilopochtli, who demanded so much sacrifice. And she appeared standing on the crescent moon, the image of another of their gods. She—and the One she bears in her womb—are more powerful than any evil in the world, more powerful than any evil in your life.

Questions for reflection:

1. *How have you tended to think about evil and the origin of evil, in the world and in your own life?*

2. *Which of the Enemy's tactics do you discover most frequently in your own life? What can you do to resist them?*

3. *Where do you need Our Lady to bring Jesus to you to overcome the power of the Enemy in your life right now?*

Action: Place an image of Our Lady of Guadalupe as the backdrop on your phone or computer, or print an image and place it somewhere you will see it throughout this day.

FRIDAY, DECEMBER 13
"If you would hearken to my commandments."

A reading from the book of the Prophet Isaiah (48:17-19)

Thus says the LORD, your redeemer,
the Holy One of Israel:
I, the LORD, your God,
teach you what is for your good,
and lead you on the way you should go.
If you would hearken to my commandments,
your prosperity would be like a river,
and your vindication like the waves of the sea;
Your descendants would be like the sand,
and those born of your stock like its grains,
Their name never cut off
or blotted out from my presence.

Responsorial Psalm (1:1-2, 3, 4 and 6)

R. **Those who follow you, Lord, will have the light of life.**

Blessed the man who follows not
the counsel of the wicked
Nor walks in the way of sinners,
nor sits in the company of the insolent,
But delights in the law of the LORD
and meditates on his law day and night. R.

He is like a tree
planted near running water,
That yields its fruit in due season,
and whose leaves never fade.
Whatever he does, prospers. R.

Not so the wicked, not so;
they are like chaff which the wind drives away.
For the LORD watches over the way of the just,
but the way of the wicked vanishes. R.

A reading from the holy Gospel according to Matthew
(11:16-19)

Jesus said to the crowds:
"To what shall I compare this generation?
It is like children who sit in marketplaces and call to
   one another,
'We played the flute for you, but you did not dance,
we sang a dirge but you did not mourn.'
For John came neither eating nor drinking, and they
   said,
'He is possessed by a demon.'
The Son of Man came eating and drinking and they
   said,
'Look, he is a glutton and a drunkard,
a friend of tax collectors and sinners.'
But wisdom is vindicated by her works."

We listen to a lot of things each day: playlists, pod-
casts, commercials, YouTube videos, TikTok, Netflix.
And we hear a lot of things we don't pay so much attention to as well: the music at the grocery store, commercials, conversations, birdsong, traffic, electronic
noises, the wind...

Everything we listen to, everything we hear, is sending us
some kind of message, telling us something about who
we are or what we should do, or who we are and how we
should be. Some of the messages we hear are like the

children sitting in the marketplace that Jesus describes in the Gospel. Some of them are insistent, coming from all around us, bombarding us.

So it's worth our while to slow down, to pay attention, to listen to what I hear and to think about what I listen to. What am I being told about myself, about others, about God? What am I being told about the meaning of life and my own place in this world? Whose voice is speaking to me through the things I choose to watch and the things I choose to listen to? Whose voice is speaking to me through the things I hear, and what impact do those things have on me?

In the end, there is only one voice that can speak the truth, only one voice that teaches what is for our good. But so often, we let His voice get drowned out by the lies of the Enemy in our hearts, or the distortions of our own desires, or the clamor of the contemporary culture, or so many other things we let fill our hearts and our minds.

If only we would hearken to God's commandments, we would learn what is for our good, and we would let Him lead us on the way we should go, on the path of true freedom and eternal happiness. But too often, we listen to the voice of the Enemy. We let him deceive us, convince us that God's commandments are taking away our freedom, that God is not really a good Father, that God is not going to give us what we need. We let him tell us that we are worthless, broken, unlovable, a burden, or whatever lies it is he speaks in your soul.

Today, let's stop and listen. Let's distinguish between the many things we hear. Let's listen for the voice of the

Lord. And let's stop listening to the other voices, the ones through which the Enemy still speaks to our souls.

Questions for reflection:

1. *What things do you deliberately listen to each day? What are the messages they speak to you about who you are, about who God is? How do they compare to what the Lord Himself says?*

2. *What are the lies that the Enemy most often speaks to your heart about God and about you? How do you habitually respond to those lies? What can you do to change any response that leads to sin?*

3. *In what ways does the Lord speak to you each day? In what ways do you make time to listen to Him?*

Action: At the end of your day today, make a list of all the different things you deliberately listened to, and what messages they were sending you. Then ask the Lord to reveal to you what and how He spoke to you this day, and write down whatever He told you.

A reading from the book of the Prophet Sirach
(48:1-4, 9-11)

In those days,
like a fire there appeared the prophet Elijah
whose words were as a flaming furnace.
Their staff of bread he shattered,
in his zeal he reduced them to straits;
By the Lord's word he shut up the heavens
and three times brought down fire.
How awesome are you, Elijah, in your wondrous deeds!
Whose glory is equal to yours?
You were taken aloft in a whirlwind of fire,
in a chariot with fiery horses.
You were destined, it is written, in time to come
to put an end to wrath before the day of the LORD,
To turn back the hearts of fathers toward their sons,
and to re-establish the tribes of Jacob.
Blessed is he who shall have seen you
and who falls asleep in your friendship.

Responsorial Psalm (80:2ac and 3b, 15-16, 18-19)

R. **Lord, make us turn to you; let us see your face
and we shall be saved.**

O shepherd of Israel, hearken,
From your throne upon the cherubim, shine forth.
Rouse your power. R.

Once again, O LORD of hosts,
look down from heaven, and see;

Take care of this vine,
and protect what your right hand has planted,
the son of man whom you yourself made strong. R.

May your help be with the man of your right hand,
with the son of man whom you yourself made strong.
Then we will no more withdraw from you;
give us new life, and we will call upon your name. R.

A reading from the holy Gospel according to Matthew
(17:9a, 10-13)

As they were coming down from the mountain,
the disciples asked Jesus,
"Why do the scribes say that Elijah must come first?"
He said in reply, "Elijah will indeed come and restore
    all things;
but I tell you that Elijah has already come,
and they did not recognize him but did to him what-
    ever they pleased.
So also will the Son of Man suffer at their hands."
Then the disciples understood
that he was speaking to them of John the Baptist.

When we read the story of the Fall carefully, we see that
among the ways the Enemy distorts the truth is his distor-
tion about what is for our highest good, the elevation of
lower desires, the insistence that we need to have pleasure and comfort—spiritually, physically, and emotion-
ally—in order to be truly happy, and that we deserve such
things and should ensure for ourselves that we have them.

We notice this if we read carefully how Genesis describes Eve's response to temptation: "The woman saw

that the tree was good for food, pleasing to the eyes, and desirable for gaining wisdom. So she took some of its fruit and ate it." She sees that it is good for food—it will fill her physically. It is pleasing to the eye—it causes her pleasure. It is desirable for gaining wisdom—it promises knowledge and control.

One of the consequences of the fall is that we have thus inherited an internal disorder that is hard to overcome. We put physical pleasure or comfort before the joys of the spiritual life, which often require sacrifice and abnegation. We put aesthetics in the place of true beauty, creating mirages of pretty things that are shallow or empty when approached for more. And we put our own knowledge, our own opinion, in the place of the truth that can set us free.

And when we do this, when we elevate our lower desires to the central place, we end up doing to others not what we would have them do to us, but whatever we please, whatever will keep them from encroaching upon our own pleasure or comfort.

Like the leaders in Jesus' day, we, too, tend to block out or silence voices that make us uncomfortable, that call us to higher things, that remind us to follow God's law.

But when we silence the voice of truth, whether from our own conscience, from Scripture, from the Church, or from those around us, we become a danger to ourselves and to others, like the leaders in Jesus' day, who, for the sake of their own sense of well-being, did to John the Baptist whatever they pleased, that is, killed him to justify themselves.

Questions for reflection:

1. *In what ways do you experience that your desires are distorted, that things are out of order within you?*

2. *How do you seek pleasure or comfort for yourself over and above the call to radical holiness?*

3. *In what ways do you seek to silence the voices of those who make you uncomfortable, who call you to follow Christ more closely? How do you silence those voices?*

Action: Write in a place where you will see it today, "Speak, Lord, your servant is listening."

WEEK THREE

RESCUED

After spending a whole week looking at sin and the effects of sin in our own lives, we are ready for salvation. After recognizing our various enslavements, we know our need for a Redeemer, someone who can come and set us free, who can break the chains, who can silence the lies, who can come down into the pit with us and lift us out to freedom.

In this last full week of Advent, we will meditate on different aspects of how Jesus has come to rescue us, preparing our hearts for Christmas, opening them so that the Christ child, who is also the eternal Son of God, can enter in and bring us true freedom and new life.

SUNDAY, DECEMBER 15

"The Lord, your God, is in your midst, a mighty savior."

A reading from the Book of the Prophet Zephaniah (3:14-18a)

Shout for joy, O daughter Zion!
  Sing joyfully, O Israel!
Be glad and exult with all your heart,
  O daughter Jerusalem!
The LORD has removed the judgment against you
  he has turned away your enemies;
the King of Israel, the LORD, is in your midst,
  you have no further misfortune to fear.
On that day, it shall be said to Jerusalem:
  Fear not, O Zion, be not discouraged!
The LORD, your God, is in your midst,
  a mighty savior;
he will rejoice over you with gladness,
  and renew you in his love,
he will sing joyfully because of you,
  as one sings at festivals.

Responsorial Psalm (Isaiah 12:2-3, 4, 5-6)

R. **Cry out with joy and gladness: for among you is the great and Holy One of Israel.**

God indeed is my savior;
  I am confident and unafraid.
My strength and my courage is the LORD,
  and he has been my savior.
With joy you will draw water
  at the fountain of salvation. R.

Give thanks to the LORD, acclaim his name;
  among the nations make known his deeds,
  proclaim how exalted is his name. R.

Sing praise to the LORD for his glorious achievement;
  let this be known throughout all the earth.
Shout with exultation, O city of Zion,
  for great in your midst
  is the Holy One of Israel! R.

A reading from the Letter of St. Paul to the Philippians
(4:4-7)

Brothers and sisters:
Rejoice in the Lord always.
I shall say it again: rejoice!
Your kindness should be known to all.
The Lord is near.
Have no anxiety at all, but in everything,
by prayer and petition, with thanksgiving,
make your requests known to God.
Then the peace of God that surpasses all understanding
will guard your hearts and minds in Christ Jesus.

A reading from the holy Gospel according to Luke
(3:10-18)

The crowds asked John the Baptist,
"What should we do?"
He said to them in reply,
"Whoever has two cloaks
should share with the person who has none.
And whoever has food should do likewise."
Even tax collectors came to be baptized and they
  said to him,
"Teacher, what should we do?"

He answered them,
"Stop collecting more than what is prescribed."
Soldiers also asked him,
"And what is it that we should do?"
He told them,
"Do not practice extortion,
do not falsely accuse anyone,
and be satisfied with your wages."

Now the people were filled with expectation,
and all were asking in their hearts
whether John might be the Christ.
John answered them all, saying,
"I am baptizing you with water,
but one mightier than I is coming.
I am not worthy to loosen the thongs of his sandals.
He will baptize you with the Holy Spirit and fire.
His winnowing fan is in his hand to clear his threshing
    floor
and to gather the wheat into his barn,
but the chaff he will burn with unquenchable fire."
Exhorting them in many other ways,
he preached good news to the people.

Some time ago, a film came out parodying Catholicism, and the one lasting image from that film, which is still all over the internet, is a ridiculous-looking statue of Jesus, "Buddy Jesus," who is winking and giving the two-thumbs-up sign, with a big goofy grin on his face. It's not a very inspiring image, to say the least. Buddy Jesus looks like he might jump on his skateboard and ride away the minute there were any threat of danger. Or there are the many soft and delicate images of Jesus, where He looks a little too weak to do anything much to save anyone.

Yes, Jesus is our friend. Yes, Jesus enjoyed spending time with His friends, and He probably did the first-century Palestine equivalent of our thumbs' up with those friends now and then. But He wasn't goofy, and He certainly wasn't weak and pale or afraid of danger.

He walked miles and miles to get from one place to another. He spent the first 30 years of His life working as a carpenter. He walked His disciples right up to the place known as "The Gates of Hell." He faced controversy without backing down, preached in a way that provoked the anger of others, challenged authority when it was misused, commanded a storm to stop, told the dead to get up and they did.

When we emphasize His compassion and His tenderness, sometimes we forget His power. But He was—and is—the all-powerful God of heaven and earth. He came to rescue us, came to overthrow the rule of the Enemy, came to destroy sin and death forever. He is a *mighty* savior. That is to say, He is *powerful*. No one and nothing can withstand His power. Not even sin. Not even Satan. Not even death.

Wherever you are weak or powerless today, know that you have a *mighty* Savior coming to your rescue. Wherever you feel defenseless or alone, know that the Lord, your God, is in your midst. Wherever you are under attack by the Enemy, know that "the Lord has removed the judgment against you, he has turned away your enemies."

He is your Friend, and so much more than your friend. He is your Teacher, and so much more than your teacher. He is tender and mighty, gentle and powerful, strong to save, able to break every chain—to destroy every weapon that is fashioned against you. And He has come for you. Wherever you need Him today, He is coming to rescue you.

Questions for reflection:

1. *What images of Jesus help you to see Him as mighty and powerful? What difference does recognizing His power make in your life?*

2. *Where do you need the Lord to manifest His might in your life right now?*

3. *What false or partial images make it difficult for you to see the Lord as powerful and to trust in His power?*

Action: Find and print an image of Jesus as a mighty savior, an image that speaks to you of His power to rescue you, and put it in a place where you will see it throughout the day.

What is offered below is a suggestion for how a priest or deacon may choose to preach the kerygma this week based on *The Rescue Project*. Last week we looked at the question "Why is everything so obviously messed up?" and the word Captured. This week we focus on the question "What, if anything, has God done about it?" and the word Rescued.

3rd Sunday of Advent
Part Three: Rescued

Ask God for the grace of unshakable confidence in Jesus as Lord of heaven and earth

Key Themes: Again, any of these are worth exploring this week. The key is to ask the Lord what is most significant for your particular community!

- God's response to our hopeless situation is shocking and unexpected.

- Why did the Son of God become man? To rescue us.

- What was Jesus doing on the cross? Showing us the Father's love; making atonement for our sins; going to war to rescue us from the enemy.

- The Passion of Jesus does not "happen" to Jesus. He wills it. Jesus on the cross is both victim and aggressor; both hunted and hunting. On the cross Jesus is like an "ambush predator": a creature that lies motionless and still, camouflaged with its environment, trying to attract prey.

- What difference does all of this make? Jesus has humiliated the enemy; destroyed the power of Death; transferred us out of darkness and into the Kingdom of God; given us access to the

Father; recreated us; rendered the power of Sin impotent; and given us authority over the enemy.

Questions for Reflection:

- How does knowing Jesus is hunting on the cross change the way you see the passion?

- When you hear about "the love of God," do you hear a trite expression, or do those words have a deeper meaning now for you?

- Do you believe you're worth fighting for and dying for to God?

Possible Verses for Focus from Today's Readings:

Zephaniah (3:14-18a): "Shout for joy, O daughter Zion! / Sing joyfully, O Israel! / Be glad and exult with all your heart, O daughter Jerusalem! / The LORD has removed the judgment against you, / he has turned away your enemies; / the King of Israel, the LORD, is in your midst, you have no further misfortune to fear. / On that day, it shall be said to Jerusalem: / Fear not, O Zion, be not discouraged! / The LORD, your God, is in your midst, / a mighty savior; / he will rejoice over you with gladness, / and renew you in his love, / he will sing joyfully because of you, / as one sings at festivals."

[Who are these "enemies?" Sin, Death, and Satan. We have been delivered, rescued, from them not by an angel or some other figure but by the Lord "in our midst" fighting out of love for us by name. God is a Savior! A Rescuer!]

Isaiah (12:2-6): "God indeed is my savior; / I am confident and unafraid... / Sing praise to the LORD for his glorious achievement; let this be known throughout all the earth. / Shout with exultation, O city of Zion."

[Once again, we see who God is: a Savior! God who is love, acts! He saves! He intervenes! He gets personally involved! To deliver us. And our response is—or should be— unbridled joy and delight!]

Philippians (4:6): "Have no anxiety at all."

[No anxiety?! Why? How? Because the gospel is the extraordinary news that we matter to God! Our lives are not in the hands of circumstances but in the hands of a good Father who has not only created us but shared with us His Son who has rescued us from those powers we could never defeat on our own. This is not to naively think that nothing bad will ever happen to us. It is instead to trust in God that no matter what happens to us He will always be with us and will give us the grace we need when we need it.]

Luke (3:15-18): "Now the people were filled with expectation, and all were asking in their hearts whether John might be the Christ. John answered them all, saying, 'I am baptizing you with water, but one mightier than I is coming. I am not worthy to loosen the thongs of his sandals. He will baptize you with the Holy Spirit and fire. His winnowing fan is in his hand to clear his threshing floor and to gather the wheat into his barn, but the chaff he will burn with unquenchable fire.' Exhorting them in many other ways, he preached good news to the people."

[What is the "good news"? That God has rescued us from futility, from slavery, from despair, from emptiness; that we matter and are loved far more than we could ever dare to imagine. Jesus is "the Messiah," meaning "the anointed one." The Jewish people had expected the Messiah to

deliver them from their enemies, and they were right. However, they were wrong in their identification of the enemy with a political power. Though Rome was in fact oppressing them, the real enemy was the devil, and he was oppressing the entire human race. Jesus, the Messiah, has defeated—though not yet destroyed—him.]

NOTES

NOTES

NOTES

NOTES

A reading from the Book of Numbers (24:2-7, 15-17a)

When Balaam raised his eyes and saw Israel encamp-
ed, tribe by tribe,
the spirit of God came upon him,
and he gave voice to his oracle:
The utterance of Balaam, son of Beor,
the utterance of a man whose eye is true,
The utterance of one who hears what God says,
and knows what the Most High knows,
Of one who sees what the Almighty sees,
enraptured, and with eyes unveiled:
How goodly are your tents, O Jacob;
your encampments, O Israel!
They are like gardens beside a stream,
like the cedars planted by the LORD.
His wells shall yield free-flowing waters,
he shall have the sea within reach;
His king shall rise higher,
and his royalty shall be exalted.
Then Balaam gave voice to his oracle:
The utterance of Balaam, son of Beor,
the utterance of the man whose eye is true,
The utterance of one who hears what God says,
and knows what the Most High knows,
Of one who sees what the Almighty sees,
enraptured, and with eyes unveiled.
I see him, though not now;
I behold him, though not near:
A star shall advance from Jacob,
and a staff shall rise from Israel.

R. **Teach me your ways, O Lord.**

Your ways, O LORD, make known to me;
    teach me your paths,
Guide me in your truth and teach me,
    for you are God my savior. R.

Remember that your compassion, O LORD,
    and your kindness are from of old.
In your kindness remember me,
    because of your goodness, O LORD. R.

Good and upright is the LORD;
    thus he shows sinners the way.
He guides the humble to justice,
    he teaches the humble his way. R.

A reading from the holy Gospel according to Matthew
(21:23-27)

When Jesus had come into the temple area,
the chief priests and the elders of the people
    approached him
as he was teaching and said,
"By what authority are you doing these things?
And who gave you this authority?"
Jesus said to them in reply,
"I shall ask you one question, and if you answer it for me,
then I shall tell you by what authority I do these things.
Where was John's baptism from?
Was it of heavenly or of human origin?"
They discussed this among themselves and said,
"If we say 'Of heavenly origin,' he will say to us,
'Then why did you not believe him?'

But if we say, 'Of human origin,' we fear the crowd,
for they all regard John as a prophet."
So they said to Jesus in reply, "We do not know."
He himself said to them,
"Neither shall I tell you by what authority I do these
  things."

When someone writes a story, that person becomes an author. No one else can rewrite it, take characters out, change the story line, rearrange the chapters, add or take away dialogue. Only the author has authority over his or her own story.

So when the Jewish leaders question Jesus about His authority, they are revealing precisely that they do not know who He is, they do not recognize that He is the Author of life, that He has, because of His divinity, absolute Authority over the Law, over nature, and even over us. They question Him because He acts in ways that scandalize them, because He is not bound to their meticulous and particularized interpretations of the law that He authored, but acts with authority over that law.

It's easy to forget that Jesus has all authority because He is the Author. Sometimes, we fall prey to the Enemy's lie that there are areas in our lives today or events in our lives in the past where the Enemy is the author, where the Lord Jesus doesn't have authority. We can believe that we are condemned to a certain pattern of thinking, to repeat a certain sin, to remain stuck in an unhealthy habit, because we forget that Jesus is the only One who really has authority over our lives, and therefore don't give Him the freedom to move and act in our lives as the Author, but instead live under the lie of the Enemy.

The authority Jesus has is absolute. He can say to the storm, "Be still," and the wind and the waves calm down. He can say to the paralytic, "Rise up and walk," and the paralytic stands up and begins walking on his once-withered legs. He can say to the deaf-mute, "Be opened," and he can suddenly speak and hear. And He can say to you, to whatever your impediment or sin or weakness or incapacity is, whatever command you need to hear for that thing in your life to be transformed.

He is, after all, the Author. He is the only one with legitimate authority in your life. And what He says changes things. His word creates, casts out, heals, forgives, restores, re-creates. So let Him speak His word of authority in your life today, and watch to see what happens.

Questions for reflection:

1. *What are the lies the Enemy tells you about the Lord's authority in your life? Where do you believe that Jesus doesn't have power to change you? Renounce that false belief.*

2. *What do you need the Lord to command to be transformed in your life today?*

3. *When you come to Scripture, do you believe that the words of the Lord in Scripture have power to transform you today? Why or why not?*

Action: Draw a book cover, title it with your name: _____'s Life Story, and put Jesus' name as the author. Keep it with you today, and look at it when you feel like there are things that can't be changed.

A reading from the Book of Genesis (49:2, 8-10)

Jacob called his sons and said to them:
"Assemble and listen, sons of Jacob,
　　listen to Israel, your father.

"You, Judah, shall your brothers praise
　　–your hand on the neck of your enemies;
　　the sons of your father shall bow down to you.
Judah, like a lion's whelp,
　　you have grown up on prey, my son.
He crouches like a lion recumbent,
　　the king of beasts–who would dare rouse him?
The scepter shall never depart from Judah,
　　or the mace from between his legs,
While tribute is brought to him,
　　and he receives the people's homage."

Responsorial Psalm (72:1-2, 3-4ab, 7-8, 17)

R. **Justice shall flourish in his time, and fullness of peace for ever.**

O God, with your judgment endow the king,
　　and with your justice, the king's son;
He shall govern your people with justice
　　and your afflicted ones with judgment. R.

The mountains shall yield peace for the people,
　　and the hills justice.
He shall defend the afflicted among the people,
　　save the children of the poor. R.

Justice shall flower in his days,
　　and profound peace, till the moon be no more.

May he rule from sea to sea,
    and from the River to the ends of the earth. R.

May his name be blessed forever;
    as long as the sun his name shall remain.
In him shall all the tribes of the earth be blessed;
    all the nations shall proclaim his happiness. R.

A reading from the holy Gospel according to Matthew
(1:1-17)

The book of the genealogy of Jesus Christ,
the son of David, the son of Abraham.

Abraham became the father of Isaac,
Isaac the father of Jacob,
Jacob the father of Judah and his brothers.
Judah became the father of Perez and Zerah,
whose mother was Tamar.
Perez became the father of Hezron,
Hezron the father of Ram,
Ram the father of Amminadab.
Amminadab became the father of Nahshon,
Nahshon the father of Salmon,
Salmon the father of Boaz,
whose mother was Rahab.
Boaz became the father of Obed,
whose mother was Ruth.
Obed became the father of Jesse,
Jesse the father of David the king.

David became the father of Solomon,
whose mother had been the wife of Uriah.
Solomon became the father of Rehoboam,
Rehoboam the father of Abijah,
Abijah the father of Asaph.

Asaph became the father of Jehoshaphat,
Jehoshaphat the father of Joram,
Joram the father of Uzziah.
Uzziah became the father of Jotham,
Jotham the father of Ahaz,
Ahaz the father of Hezekiah.
Hezekiah became the father of Manasseh,
Manasseh the father of Amos,
Amos the father of Josiah.
Josiah became the father of Jechoniah and his
    brothers
at the time of the Babylonian exile.

After the Babylonian exile,
Jechoniah became the father of Shealtiel,
Shealtiel the father of Zerubbabel,
Zerubbabel the father of Abiud.
Abiud became the father of Eliakim,
Eliakim the father of Azor,
Azor the father of Zadok.
Zadok became the father of Achim,
Achim the father of Eliud,
Eliud the father of Eleazar.
Eleazar became the father of Matthan,
Matthan the father of Jacob,
Jacob the father of Joseph, the husband of Mary.
Of her was born Jesus who is called the Christ.

Thus the total number of generations
from Abraham to David
is fourteen generations;
from David to the Babylonian exile, fourteen
    generations;
from the Babylonian exile to the Christ,
fourteen generations.

In Jerusalem, in the Church of the Holy Sepulchre, right below the chapel of Calvary, where the Cross of Christ stood, is the chapel of Adam's Tomb. Tradition tells us that Adam and Eve were buried there, under what later became the place of the crucifixion of Jesus, and that when the earthquake happened at the moment of Jesus' death, the blood of Christ flowed down the fissure created in the bedrock of Calvary, down onto Adam's bones.

It's a powerful place to pray, to contemplate the reach of redemption. Jesus' death on the Cross didn't just overcome sin and death for those who came after Him. No, from the Cross and in the Resurrection, Jesus reaches all the way back to the beginning of human history, to the very first people who ever lived, to overcome even that first sin and the wound of original sin—to set our ancestors free.

That's part of what this genealogy tells us. When the Son of God came into this world in the Incarnation, when He lived a human life, suffered and died for us on the cross, then rose again on the third day, that wasn't just for the people living at His time and for those of us who came after. It was for everyone who has ever lived, everyone who has ever turned to God and trusted in God.

And it's not only that Jesus reaches back to the beginning of human history and to the end of it, but that His work of redemption, His rescue of fallen, captured humanity, reaches all the way back to the beginning of your life and of my life. There is nothing in our lives that cannot be transformed by the Blood of Jesus Christ. As He dies on the Cross for us, He takes upon Himself, absorbs into Himself, all of your sins and all of my sins, all of your wounds and all of my wounds, from the beginning of our lives until the day we see Him face to face in glory.

There is no sin in your past that His blood doesn't forgive. There is no wound in your soul that His love won't heal. There is no fall in your future where His Cross won't be victorious. Nothing, absolutely nothing, in your history or in my history is beyond the reach of His redemption.

Questions for reflection:

1. *What events or experiences in your early life do you need the Lord to touch with His work of redemption? Expose them to Him.*

2. *Where in your personal history have you already experienced that Jesus has rescued you? From what?*

3. *How has the Lord transformed something in your life that was for you a cause of shame or suffering into a means of grace?*

Action: Draw a timeline of your life that includes the major ways sin has wounded you (either your own or others' sins) and the ways that Jesus has already intervened in your life.

"He will save his people from their sins."

A reading from the Book of the Prophet Jerimiah
(23:5-8)

Behold, the days are coming, says the LORD,
when I will raise up a righteous shoot to David;
As king he shall reign and govern wisely,
he shall do what is just and right in the land.
In his days Judah shall be saved,
Israel shall dwell in security.
This is the name they give him:
"The LORD our justice."

Therefore, the days will come, says the LORD,
when they shall no longer say, "As the LORD lives,
who brought the children of Israel out of the land of
    Egypt";
but rather, "As the LORD lives,
who brought the descendants of the house of Israel
up from the land of the north"–
and from all the lands to which I banished them;
they shall again live on their own land.

Responsorial Psalm (72:1-2, 12-13, 18-19)

R. **Justice shall flourish in his time, and fullness of
peace for ever.**

O God, with your judgment endow the king,
and with your justice, the king's son;
He shall govern your people with justice
and your afflicted ones with judgment. R.

For he shall rescue the poor when he cries out,

and the afflicted when he has no one to help him.
He shall have pity for the lowly and the poor;
the lives of the poor he shall save. R.

Blessed be the LORD, the God of Israel,
who alone does wondrous deeds.
And blessed forever be his glorious name;
may the whole earth be filled with his glory. R.

A reading from the holy Gospel according to Matthew
(1:18-25)

This is how the birth of Jesus Christ came about.
When his mother Mary was betrothed to Joseph,
but before they lived together,
she was found with child through the Holy Spirit.
Joseph her husband, since he was a righteous man,
yet unwilling to expose her to shame,
decided to divorce her quietly.
Such was his intention when, behold,
the angel of the Lord appeared to him in a dream and
    said,
"Joseph, son of David,
do not be afraid to take Mary your wife into your home.
For it is through the Holy Spirit
that this child has been conceived in her.
She will bear a son and you are to name him Jesus,
because he will save his people from their sins."
All this took place to fulfill
what the Lord had said through the prophet:

Behold, the virgin shall be with child and bear a son,
and they shall name him Emmanuel,
which means "God is with us."
When Joseph awoke,

he did as the angel of the Lord had commanded him
and took his wife into his home.
He had no relations with her until she bore a son,
and he named him Jesus.

Sometimes we have a pretty shallow idea of sin and its consequences. We go to confession as if it were a routine step we need to take, a kind of checkpoint on the way to Holy Communion. Or we think about sin in terms of bad behavior and punishment, a sort of legal retribution system, as if the laws we break when we sin were of no more importance than a minor traffic violation. But if that were the case, why would we need a savior?

What happens when we go to the Sacrament of Confession is not a mere legal technicality, not a simple ritual, not a mere removal of guilt. It is an act of *salvation*, an act of *rescue*.

And that's partly why it's so important for us to ask the Holy Spirit for the grace of true contrition—that is, true and deep sorrow for our sins. (Who can feel truly and deeply sorry for going 40 in a 35 mph zone?) If I don't understand the reality of what I've done, if I don't understand the real weight of my sins, if I don't realize that I am bound in chains too heavy for me to break, chains that are pulling me lower and lower, then how can I recognize in the confessional the incredible saving action of Jesus Christ through the words of absolution spoken by the priest?

The people of Israel at the time of Jesus recognized that their oppression by the Romans, after decades of exile and oppression by other peoples, was a result of their sins. They were waiting for a savior, waiting for the Anointed One to come and set them free.

My own enslavement, your own oppression, they are the result of our sins. We are desperately in need of a Savior, of a Redeemer, of someone who can come in and break these chains, who can overthrow the powers of sin and death, who can pull us out of darkness, who can clothe us and restore us to our right mind and our true identity.

And that is what happens each time we go to confession. We don't just recite our sins and receive some advice and hear some ritual formula of absolution. We go in chained and oppressed, condemned to death, and we come out free from the chains, acquitted of all guilt, set on a new pathway of life.

So let's ask the Holy Spirit to reveal to us the real gravity of our sins. Let's ask Him to pull back the curtain and show us the spiritual reality of the chains we wear, the oppression we suffer, so that when we go to confession again, we can also see the reality of Jesus, saving us from our sin.

Questions for reflection:

1. *What sins do you commit that seem to you unimportant? Why do you think of them as unimportant?*

2. *How do you approach the Sacrament of Confession?*

3. *When have you experienced a real need for confession? When have you experienced the Lord truly setting you free through this sacrament?*

Action: Prepare your confession, using your notes from the meditations in this booklet up to today.

A reading from the Book of Judges (13:2-7, 24-25a)

There was a certain man from Zorah, of the clan of
the Danites,
whose name was Manoah.
His wife was barren and had borne no children.
An angel of the LORD appeared to the woman and
said to her,
"Though you are barren and have had no children,
yet you will conceive and bear a son.
Now, then, be careful to take no wine or strong drink
and to eat nothing unclean.
As for the son you will conceive and bear,
no razor shall touch his head,
for this boy is to be consecrated to God from the womb.
It is he who will begin the deliverance of Israel
from the power of the Philistines."

The woman went and told her husband,
"A man of God came to me;
he had the appearance of an angel of God, terrible
indeed.
I did not ask him where he came from, nor did he tell
me his name.
But he said to me,
'You will be with child and will bear a son.
So take neither wine nor strong drink, and eat noth-
ing unclean.
For the boy shall be consecrated to God from the womb,
until the day of his death.'"

The woman bore a son and named him Samson.

The boy grew up and the LORD blessed him;
the Spirit of the LORD stirred him.

R. **My mouth shall be filled with your praise, and I will
sing your glory!**

Be my rock of refuge,
a stronghold to give me safety,
for you are my rock and my fortress.
O my God, rescue me from the hand of the wicked. R.

For you are my hope, O LORD;
my trust, O God, from my youth.
On you I depend from birth;
from my mother's womb you are my strength. R.

I will treat of the mighty works of the LORD;
O God, I will tell of your singular justice.
O God, you have taught me from my youth,
and till the present I proclaim your wondrous deeds. R.

A reading from the holy Gospel according to Luke
(1:5-25)

In the days of Herod, King of Judea,
there was a priest named Zechariah
of the priestly division of Abijah;
his wife was from the daughters of Aaron,
and her name was Elizabeth.
Both were righteous in the eyes of God,
observing all the commandments
and ordinances of the Lord blamelessly.
But they had no child, because Elizabeth was barren
and both were advanced in years.

Once when he was serving as priest
in his division's turn before God,
according to the practice of the priestly service,
he was chosen by lot
to enter the sanctuary of the Lord to burn incense.
Then, when the whole assembly of the people was
   praying outside
at the hour of the incense offering,
the angel of the Lord appeared to him,
standing at the right of the altar of incense.
Zechariah was troubled by what he saw, and fear
   came upon him.

But the angel said to him, "Do not be afraid,
   Zechariah,
because your prayer has been heard.
Your wife Elizabeth will bear you a son,
and you shall name him John.
And you will have joy and gladness,
and many will rejoice at his birth,
for he will be great in the sight of the Lord.
He will drink neither wine nor strong drink.
He will be filled with the Holy Spirit even from his
   mother's womb,
and he will turn many of the children of Israel
to the Lord their God.
He will go before him in the spirit and power of Elijah
to turn the hearts of fathers toward children
and the disobedient to the understanding of the
   righteous,
to prepare a people fit for the Lord."

Then Zechariah said to the angel,
"How shall I know this?
For I am an old man, and my wife is advanced in years."

And the angel said to him in reply,
"I am Gabriel, who stand before God.
I was sent to speak to you and to announce to you
    this good news.
But now you will be speechless and unable to talk
until the day these things take place,
because you did not believe my words,
which will be fulfilled at their proper time."
Meanwhile the people were waiting for Zechariah
and were amazed that he stayed so long in the
    sanctuary.
But when he came out, he was unable to speak to them,
and they realized that he had seen a vision in the
    sanctuary.
He was gesturing to them but remained mute.

Then, when his days of ministry were completed, he
    went home.

After this time his wife Elizabeth conceived,
and she went into seclusion for five months, saying,
"So has the Lord done for me at a time when he has
    seen fit
to take away my disgrace before others."

One of the most striking things about the story of the Fall in Genesis is the immediate action of Adam and Eve to cover themselves, to hide themselves, after they eat of the fruit. Before that, Scripture tells us, they "were naked and felt no shame." They could just be who they were, unashamed, because they were pure, holy, exactly who they had been created to be. Nothing was missing that should be there, and nothing was there that shouldn't be. But as soon as they fall, even before God speaks to them, they experience shame.

And because of that shame, they try to cover them-selves up, to protect themselves from one another. And then they hide from God, not wanting Him to see them now, convinced that they are now unlovable, unaccept-able, rejected.

We can experience shame—which is a feeling or belief that one is unworthy of being loved and unlovable—be-cause of things we've done, because of things others have done to us, or because of situations in life. It can be a crippling wound to deal with, because it constantly tells us that we are not good enough, that we cannot be loved, that we are deeply and irreparably unworthy.

When Jesus comes to set us free, He doesn't just re-move the guilt of our sin. He comes to set us free from shame, too, to restore in us the sense of being beloved by God, chosen by Him, worthy of love.

That is what happens with Elizabeth. She has lived her whole married life with the shame of being unable to con-ceive a child, of being barren, in a time and in a culture when children were seen as a blessing from the Lord, and barrenness was seen as being somehow one's own fault. When she conceives, her response is, "He has seen fit to take away my disgrace before others."

He has seen fit to take away my disgrace, to take away my shame. And He has seen fit to take away your dis-grace, your shame, to clothe you anew in robes of salva-tion, to place new sandals on your feet and a ring on your finger, to call you His beloved child. You are who He says you are, not who your wounds say you are. And you are, always and forever, His.

Questions for reflection:

1. *When have you felt most ashamed? What did you do as a result of that shame?*

2. *In what ways has the Lord already removed shame from your life?*

3. *Where do you today experience shame and need the Lord to take it away?*

Action: Find and listen to the worship song, "Who You Say I Am."

*"The Virgin shall be with child, and bear a son
and shall name him Immanuel."*

A reading from the Book of the Prophet Isaiah (7:10-14)

The LORD spoke to Ahaz:
Ask for a sign from the LORD, your God;
let it be deep as the nether world, or high as the sky!
But Ahaz answered,
"I will not ask! I will not tempt the LORD!"
Then Isaiah said:
Listen, O house of David!
Is it not enough for you to weary men,
must you also weary my God?
Therefore the Lord himself will give you this sign:
the virgin shall conceive and bear a son,
and shall name him Emmanuel.

Responsorial Psalm (24:1-2, 3-4ab, 5-6)

R. **Let the Lord enter; he is the king of glory.**

The LORD's are the earth and its fullness;
the world and those who dwell in it.
For he founded it upon the seas
and established it upon the rivers. R.

Who can ascend the mountain of the LORD?
or who may stand in his holy place?
He whose hands are sinless, whose heart is clean,
who desires not what is vain. R.

He shall receive a blessing from the LORD,
a reward from God his savior.
Such is the race that seeks for him,
that seeks the face of the God of Jacob. R.

In the sixth month,
the angel Gabriel was sent from God
to a town of Galilee called Nazareth,
to a virgin betrothed to a man named Joseph,
of the house of David,
and the virgin's name was Mary.
And coming to her, he said,
"Hail, full of grace! The Lord is with you."
But she was greatly troubled at what was said
and pondered what sort of greeting this might be.
Then the angel said to her,
"Do not be afraid, Mary,
for you have found favor with God.
Behold, you will conceive in your womb and bear a son,
and you shall name him Jesus.
He will be great and will be called Son of the Most High,
and the Lord God will give him the throne of David his
    father,
and he will rule over the house of Jacob forever,
and of his Kingdom there will be no end."

But Mary said to the angel,
"How can this be,
since I have no relations with a man?"
And the angel said to her in reply,
"The Holy Spirit will come upon you,
and the power of the Most High will overshadow you.
Therefore the child to be born
will be called holy, the Son of God.
And behold, Elizabeth, your relative,
has also conceived a son in her old age,
and this is the sixth month for her who was called barren;

for nothing will be impossible for God."

Mary said, "Behold, I am the handmaid of the Lord.
May it be done to me according to your word."
Then the angel departed from her.

The other day, I met a man outside a tire shop, and we started talking about life. I don't know what got us started, actually, how we began to converse, but he was talking about the desperate lack of meaning in all of his patients (he's a psychotherapist), and how that is at the root of the opioid crisis and so many other problems plaguing our society. So at one point, I asked him, "Are you a man of faith?" He had a hard time answering. He talked about having studied in seminary for a time, and then having studied various religions of the world, and how he encounters God when he hikes up the mountains. "God is everywhere," he said.

True, God is everywhere—all of creation has its being from Him and is somehow in Him. But to say, then, that God is with me because He is present on the mountain or in the woods or by the ocean is something quite different from saying that God is, in Christ, Immanuel. In the first, God is present in a way that is analogical to the presence of authors in their stories. In the second, God enters into the story, becomes a character in the story, becomes one of us.

In ancient mythologies, when any of the gods takes on human form, it is in order to interact with humans for a short time—and more often than not, those interactions are deceptive and self-serving on the god's part, who takes on human form in order to get something from us.

How different from the Incarnation! How opposed to the God who needs nothing, who seeks nothing from us, who wants only our eternal happiness, and so enters into this world, not disguised as a human, but really taking our nature to Himself. The Incarnation is a real historical event that in some sense changes the second Person of the Trinity forever, because when He becomes one of us, He remains one of us.

In the Incarnation, God has truly become Immanuel, God with us, God who knows what it is like to live a fully human life, God who has friends, who grows up in a human family, who works with His hands, who studies, who prays, who feels anger and sorrow, joy and trust, who faces betrayal and rejection, who is comforted by the love and hospitality of His friends. God is with us in every aspect of our lives and in every moment of our lives.

Because He has become one of us, one with us, there is no moment of our lives where He has not been present, where He has not been with us. Discovering that presence, especially in the hardest times, unleashes in our lives the healing power of His salvation.

Questions for reflection:

1. *When have you experienced that God was with you, in a personal and particular way? What was He doing in your life through that experience?*

2. *Are there moments or events in your life that you have felt you were all alone? When you present them to the Lord now in prayer, what does He want to show you about His presence with you?*

3. *In what situations in your life currently do you tend to forget that God is with you? How would you live those situations differently if you remembered His presence?*

Action: In the place where you will spend the majority of your day (your office, home, etc.), write the word "IMMANUEL" in bold lettering.

SATURDAY, DECEMBER 21
"Let me see you, let me hear your voice.
For your voice is sweet, and you are lovely."

A reading from the Song of Solomon (2:8–14)

Hark! my lover–here he comes
springing across the mountains,
leaping across the hills.
My lover is like a gazelle
or a young stag.
Here he stands behind our wall,
gazing through the windows,
peering through the lattices.
My lover speaks; he says to me,
"Arise, my beloved, my dove, my beautiful one,
and come!

"For see, the winter is past,
the rains are over and gone.
The flowers appear on the earth,
the time of pruning the vines has come,
and the song of the dove is heard in our land.
The fig tree puts forth its figs,
and the vines, in bloom, give forth fragrance.
Arise, my beloved, my beautiful one,
and come!

"O my dove in the clefts of the rock,
in the secret recesses of the cliff,
Let me see you,
let me hear your voice,
For your voice is sweet,
and you are lovely."

or

Shout for joy, O daughter Zion!
Sing joyfully, O Israel!
Be glad and exult with all your heart,
O daughter Jerusalem!
The LORD has removed the judgment against you,
he has turned away your enemies;
The King of Israel, the LORD, is in your midst,
you have no further misfortune to fear.
On that day, it shall be said to Jerusalem:
Fear not, O Zion, be not discouraged!
The LORD, your God, is in your midst,
a mighty savior;
He will rejoice over you with gladness,
and renew you in his love,
He will sing joyfully because of you,
as one sings at festivals.

Responsorial Psalm (33:2-3, 11-12, 20-21)

R. **Exult, you just, in the Lord! Sing to him a new song.**

Give thanks to the LORD on the harp;
with the ten-stringed lyre chant his praises.
Sing to him a new song;
pluck the strings skillfully, with shouts of gladness. R.

But the plan of the LORD stands forever;
the design of his heart, through all generations.
Blessed the nation whose God is the LORD,
the people he has chosen for his own inheritance. R.

Our soul waits for the LORD,
who is our help and our shield,

For in him our hearts rejoice;
in his holy name we trust. R.

Mary set out in those days
and traveled to the hill country in haste
to a town of Judah,
where she entered the house of Zechariah
and greeted Elizabeth.
When Elizabeth heard Mary's greeting,
the infant leaped in her womb,
and Elizabeth, filled with the Holy Spirit,
cried out in a loud voice and said,
"Most blessed are you among women,
and blessed is the fruit of your womb.
And how does this happen to me,
that the mother of my Lord should come to me?
For at the moment the sound of your greeting
    reached my ears,
the infant in my womb leaped for joy.
Blessed are you who believed
that what was spoken to you by the Lord
would be fulfilled."

I've always loved to sing. In fact, my mind is often a kind
of jukebox—plug a word or a phrase in, and a song comes
out. I think I've always been like that, and when I was grow-
ing up, I would sing a lot, not for anyone or anything—just
because there was a song on my mind or in my heart.

Until one day, one of my siblings told me I shouldn't. "You
don't have a good voice," she said. "You really shouldn't

sing." And from that moment on, my singing was relegated to times when I was alone, like in the car.

Then, many years later, one Saturday evening at Mass, during the greeting of peace a woman said, "You have such a beautiful voice." I was sure she was mistaken, and wanted to identify who she had heard. The people nearest me in my pew were elderly men. The people in the nearest pews behind me were also elderly men. Maybe she wasn't mistaken?

The Lord God says that to you and to me. "Your voice is sweet." And we look around for the next person, unable to believe that He wants to hear us. "You are such a delight to be with," He says, and we think, "He has no idea what a pill I am." He says, "You are lovely," and we think, "He's definitely talking to someone else."

But He's not talking to someone else. He's talking to you. He's talking to me. It's hard for us to believe, because when we look at ourselves, we see all the flaws, all the faults, all the broken places. How could He love me when this is the state I'm in? How could He, the Lord of glory, take delight in me?

I don't know how to explain it—I just know it's true. Otherwise, why would He have gone to such lengths to rescue us? His love is not impersonal, not cold, not indifferent. He didn't just rescue you so you could be okay. He rescued you because He loves you, and He wants to spend time with you. He wants to look at you, wants you to show Him your heart, to show yourself to Him. He wants to listen to your voice, which to Him is sweet. And He wants you to know that you are lovely.

So let's choose to believe this truth that is so hard for us to embrace: God loves *me*, just as I am today. He wants me to live in His presence because He delights in me.

Questions for reflection:

1. *What good thing has the Lord told you about yourself that you find hardest to accept? Why?*

2. *What stirs in your heart when you read the passage from Song of Songs and think of the Lord saying those words to you?*

3. *What difference would it make in your life right now if you were to accept that the Lord loves you just as you are and wants to spend time with you?*

Action: Today, enter into the Lord's presence and sing to Him with all your heart, either a song you already know or one you compose in the moment.

WEEK FOUR + OCTAVE OF CHRISTMAS

RESPONSE

This last week of meditations encompasses the last few days of Advent, then Christmas Day and the first days of the octave of Christmas. Until now, we have been preparing for the birth of the Christ child, reflecting on how we were created, how we were captured, what it means to have been rescued, and now, together with the Virgin Mary, early martyrs and saints, and those who first saw the newborn Savior, we are called to respond.

If we have grasped what Jesus has done for us in entering into this world to rescue us, our only response can be praise, surrender, thanksgiving, worship, and a life lived radically for Him, who lived His whole life on earth radically for us. Let's ask for the grace to respond with our whole heart, with our whole life, with our whole being. Let's ask for the grace, as we enter into Christmas, to have hearts that are open and ready, hearts that are like that manger in Bethlehem, where He can be born anew.

"Behold, I come to do Your will."

A reading from the Book of the Prophet Micah (5:1-4a)

Thus says the LORD:
You, Bethlehem-Ephrathah
    too small to be among the clans of Judah,
from you shall come forth for me
    one who is to be ruler in Israel;
whose origin is from of old,
    from ancient times.
Therefore the Lord will give them up, until the
time
    when she who is to give birth has borne,
and the rest of his kindred shall return
    to the children of Israel.
He shall stand firm and shepherd his flock
    by the strength of the LORD,
    in the majestic name of the LORD, his God;
and they shall remain, for now his greatness
    shall reach to the ends of the earth;
    he shall be peace.

Responsorial Psalm (80:2-3, 15-16, 18-19)

R. **Lord, make us turn to you; let us see your face
and we shall be saved.**

O shepherd of Israel, hearken,
    from your throne upon the cherubim, shine forth.
Rouse your power,
    and come to save us. R.

Once again, O LORD of hosts,
    look down from heaven, and see;
take care of this vine,
    and protect what your right hand has planted,
the son of man whom you yourself made strong. R.

May your help be with the man of your right hand,
    with the son of man whom you yourself made strong.
Then we will no more withdraw from you;
    give us new life, and we will call upon your name. R.

A reading from the Letter to the Hebrews (10:5-10)

Brothers and sisters:
When Christ came into the world, he said:
    "Sacrifice and offering you did not desire,
        but a body you prepared for me;
    in holocausts and sin offerings you took no delight.
    Then I said, 'As is written of me in the scroll,
    behold, I come to do your will, O God.'"

First he says, "Sacrifices and offerings,
holocausts and sin offerings,
you neither desired nor delighted in."
These are offered according to the law.
Then he says: "Behold, I come to do your will."
He takes away the first to establish the second.
By this "will," we have been consecrated
through the offering of the body of Jesus Christ once
    for all.

A reading from the holy Gospel according to Luke
(1:39-45)

Mary set out
and traveled to the hill country in haste

to a town of Judah,
where she entered the house of Zechariah
and greeted Elizabeth.
When Elizabeth heard Mary's greeting,
the infant leaped in her womb,
and Elizabeth, filled with the Holy Spirit,
cried out in a loud voice and said,
"Blessed are you among women,
and blessed is the fruit of your womb.
And how does this happen to me,
that the mother of my Lord should come to me?
For at the moment the sound of your greeting
    reached my ears,
the infant in my womb leaped for joy.
Blessed are you who believed
that what was spoken to you by the Lord
would be fulfilled."

Imagine for a moment that you are in the garden with Mary Magdalene, outside the tomb. Just a few days ago, you watched Jesus give His life for you, and as He poured out His blood on the cross, you realized that it was for you, that what He was doing as He suffered was to forgive you of your sins, to set you free. You realized in that moment, as you watched Him breathe His last, that all He had done in your life was at the price of all He was now suffering. So you have come to do for Him what you can, to anoint His body. And when He appears to you, alive—this Jesus whom you love and whom you saw die—when He says your name, all you want to do is whatever He asks you to do. In the face of so great a love, how could you not respond with love?

So when Jesus tells you, "Stop holding on to me, but go to my brothers and tell them," even though part of your heart wants to keep holding on to Him, to simply stay with Him, you run and tell the disciples, because more than you want what you feel would be best, what you think you would most enjoy, you want to do His will. You want to thank Him with your life.

When we know ourselves rescued by Jesus, when we recognize the reality of our captivity and the length He went to save us, to free us, to rescue us, then what we want is to say, "I come to do your will."

How could One who gave everything for love of you not have your best interest in mind? How could One who battled Satan and all of his armies to set you free not will your greatest good? And how could the One who created the heaven and earth, the One who created you and knows every detail about you, not know what is best for you?

The only logical thing, the only loving thing, is to respond with loving surrender, to come before Him, kneel down, and say: "Here I am, Lord Jesus, I come to do your will." Whatever that is. Your will, not mine.

We think of doing God's will as a kind of grand project for our lives—and it is, but it is also in the small details of daily life. He wills us to be faithful to the tasks at hand. He wills us to love, and love concretely, the very real persons with whom He has placed us. He wills us to live for Him, moment by moment.

Therefore, let's respond with loving surrender, not just in the big things, but in the small things of this day. Let's say to Him this morning and every morning, "Behold, I come to do your will." In small things, in big things, I come to do Your will, my King.

Questions for reflection:

1. *When you think about God's will for your life, how do you envision it? How connected is that vision to your actual, real-life situations?*

2. *What has the Lord asked of you that was different from your own plans? What did you discover about His love for you when you chose to do what He asked?*

3. *What are the daily things in which the Lord invites you to do His will today?*

Action: As you end this time of meditation today, trace the sign of the cross on your feet or legs and say, "Behold, I come to do your will," and go without delay to the next thing you need to do. Repeat throughout the day.

What is offered below is a suggestion for how a priest or deacon may choose to preach the kerygma this week based on *The Rescue Project*. Last week we looked at the question "What, if anything, has God done about it?" and the word Rescued. This week we focus on the question "How should I respond?" and the word Response.

4th Sunday of Advent
Part Four: Response

Ask for the grace of gratitude, surrender, and magnanimity.

Key Themes: Again, any of these are worth exploring this week. The key is to ask the Lord what is most significant for your particular community!

- To all that we have heard so far, a response must be made—even to put off making a decision is a response.

- No one has reasonably come close to doing for us what Jesus has done. No one else has battled Death, Sin, and Satan for us and won.

- Reasonable, intelligible, and logical responses to a God who does all that He has done in Jesus include: praising Him; thanking Him; entrusting ourselves to Him out of grateful love.

- As disciples we each have a mission in this world. That mission has an internal dimension to it (holiness) and an external dimension to it (evangelization and recreation).

- Though we cannot "build the city of God," we can build for it until the Lord returns to make all things new.

- As disciples, we are called and sent by Jesus:
  - To be in agonizing prayer on behalf of the world
  - To unite our sufferings to His for the redemption of the world
  - To be agents of sabotage and resistance
  - To be agents of recreation
  - To be agents of restoration
  - To be agents of reconciliation
  - To be agents of healing
  - To be ambassadors of God who invite others to "defect" from the kingdom of the world into the kingdom of a good Father.

Questions for Reflection:

- Do I daily consider all that Jesus has done for me?

- What is Jesus concretely asking me to do today to continue the work He began through the Incarnation?

Possible Verses for Focus from Today's Readings:

Micah (5:1-4): *[The entire passage can help us understand that God's desire is not simply that some people would be rescued and come to know the fullness of life, but that the entirety of God's creation would be under the loving rule of God.]*

Psalms (80): "Lord, make us turn to you..."

[This verse reminds us that it is OK to beg God to move in us or else all of this just remains data and information.]

Hebrews (10:5-7): "When Christ came into the world, he said: 'Sacrifice and offering you did not desire, but a body you prepared for me; in holocausts and sin offerings you took no delight. Then I said, 'As is written of me in the scroll, behold, I come to do your will, O God.'"

[What is the will of God that Hebrews is speaking of? Why has His Son come? To rescue His good creation from Sin, Death, and Satan.]

Luke (1:43-44): "And how does this happen to me, that the mother of my Lord should come to me? For at the moment the sound of your greeting reached my ears, the infant in my womb leaped for joy!"

[Mary is deserving of the highest honor we can give to any human person, for no one has done anything that compares to what Mary has done in saying yes to God's invitation to become the mother of His Son and our Rescuer. Lord is not a mere title but a reality. To say Jesus is Lord is to acknowledge nobody else is. Jesus has no rival, He has conquered the greatest of enemies: Sin, Death, and Satan, and all out of love for us. It is because of this that we don't need to be anxious or fearful, as our lives and all of history is in this Lord's hands. The response to getting near to Jesus, like John even in the womb, is joy!]

NOTES

NOTES

NOTES

*"He will sit refining and purifying silver,
and he will purify the sons of Levi,
refining them like gold or like silver."*

A reading from the Book of the Prophet Malachi
(3:1-4, 23-24)

Thus says the Lord GOD:
Lo, I am sending my messenger
to prepare the way before me;
And suddenly there will come to the temple
the LORD whom you seek,
And the messenger of the covenant whom you desire.
Yes, he is coming, says the LORD of hosts.
But who will endure the day of his coming?
And who can stand when he appears?
For he is like the refiner's fire,
or like the fuller's lye.
He will sit refining and purifying silver,
and he will purify the sons of Levi,
Refining them like gold or like silver
that they may offer due sacrifice to the LORD.
Then the sacrifice of Judah and Jerusalem
will please the LORD,
as in the days of old, as in years gone by.

Lo, I will send you
Elijah, the prophet,
Before the day of the LORD comes,
the great and terrible day,
To turn the hearts of the fathers to their children,
and the hearts of the children to their fathers,
Lest I come and strike
the land with doom.

R. **Lift up your heads and see; your redemption is near at hand.**

Your ways, O LORD, make known to me;
teach me your paths,
Guide me in your truth and teach me,
for you are God my savior. R.

Good and upright is the LORD;
thus he shows sinners the way.
He guides the humble to justice,
he teaches the humble his way. R.

All the paths of the LORD are kindness and constancy
toward those who keep his covenant and his decrees.
The friendship of the LORD is with those who fear him,
and his covenant, for their instruction. R.

A reading from the holy Gospel according to Luke
(1:57-66)

When the time arrived for Elizabeth to have her child
she gave birth to a son.
Her neighbors and relatives heard
that the Lord had shown his great mercy toward her,
and they rejoiced with her.
When they came on the eighth day to circumcise the
child,
they were going to call him Zechariah after his father,
but his mother said in reply,
"No. He will be called John."
But they answered her,
"There is no one among your relatives who has this
name."

So they made signs, asking his father what he wished
   him to be called.
He asked for a tablet and wrote, "John is his name,"
and all were amazed.
Immediately his mouth was opened, his tongue freed,
and he spoke blessing God.
Then fear came upon all their neighbors,
and all these matters were discussed
throughout the hill country of Judea.
All who heard these things took them to heart, saying,
"What, then, will this child be?"
For surely the hand of the Lord was with him.

When silver is found in a mine, it is a dark, dull gray col-
or, and it is mixed with other metals. Before the metal
is ready even to go into the fire, the rocks have to be
broken down into much smaller pieces, crushed into
pebbles or dust. Then the metal is put into a crucible,
which the silversmith takes with tongs and holds in the
hottest part of the flame. As the metal melts, it begins to
separate, and the silversmith watches the metal carefully, so he can see when it's time to pull the crucible out
of the flame and let it cool.

When it has cooled, he breaks it open to reveal the silver inside. Often, the process of melting down the metal
in the crucible over the hottest part of the fire has to be
repeated, until all the impurity is melted away, and all that
is left is the precious metal.

It's a part of our rescue, this purification. We don't
necessarily like this part so much, and tend to respond
rather poorly. Often, we're afraid of the flames, afraid
of the pain. Held out over the fire, we can feel all alone,

like God has abandoned us, and be tempted to give up, to go back to whatever it is that the Lord is purifying us from, simply because, in the process of purification, it can be hard to experience His presence, hard to remember and trust that He is there, that this is His work in us, too.

Or we can be tempted to think that we are only all that junk that keeps bubbling up, that the impurities and sinful inclinations and unhealthy attachments are what really define us.

But the Lord, our rescuer, is also our purifier. He is the one who knows what we are really made of, and He is the one who holds us in the fire, the one who carefully watches over the whole process, the one who knows when to pull us out of the flame.

He believes we are worth it. We are worth the cross, His crucible, where He has taken unto Himself all of our sinful impurities, all of our unworthiness, and burned it away in the fire of His love for us. He sees us as precious, sees us as we will be when the process is complete: pure, bright, shining, all sinfulness and impurity gone.

He doesn't get bored and go off to do something else when He holds us in the fire. No, He sits there and watches us, holding onto the crucible the whole time. He doesn't take His eyes off of us for a second. Because we are precious in His eyes, and He loves us. So let's not resist when He holds us in the flame, because the flame is the fire of His love. Let's not take ourselves out of the fire, but rather respond with surrender. My God knows what is good for me.

Questions for reflection:

1. *How have you experienced purification as part of the Lord's work of rescue in your life? How has He used times of purification to set you free?*

2. *What lies or deceptions of the Enemy come most quickly to mind when you are in the crucible? What words of the Lord can you use to combat those lies?*

3. *What does God see in you that He chooses to place you in the fire? Ask Him to show you.*

Action: Draw the Sacred Heart of Jesus, and write your name within the flames coming from the top of His Heart.

A reading from the second Book of Samuel (7:1-5, 8b-12, 14a, 16)

When King David was settled in his palace,
and the LORD had given him rest from his enemies on
    every side,
he said to Nathan the prophet,
"Here I am living in a house of cedar,
while the ark of God dwells in a tent!"
Nathan answered the king,
"Go, do whatever you have in mind,
for the LORD is with you."
But that night the LORD spoke to Nathan and said:
"Go, tell my servant David, 'Thus says the LORD:
Should you build me a house to dwell in?

"'It was I who took you from the pasture
and from the care of the flock
to be commander of my people Israel.
I have been with you wherever you went,
and I have destroyed all your enemies before you.
And I will make you famous like the great ones of the
    earth.
I will fix a place for my people Israel;
I will plant them so that they may dwell in their place
without further disturbance.
Neither shall the wicked continue to afflict them as
    they did of old,
since the time I first appointed judges over my people
    Israel.
I will give you rest from all your enemies.

The LORD also reveals to you
that he will establish a house for you.
And when your time comes and you rest with your
ancestors,
I will raise up your heir after you, sprung from your
loins,
and I will make his Kingdom firm.
I will be a father to him,
and he shall be a son to me.
Your house and your Kingdom shall endure forever
before me;
your throne shall stand firm forever.'"

Responsorial Psalm (89:2-3, 4-5, 27 and 29)

R. **For ever I will sing the goodness of the Lord.**

The favors of the LORD I will sing forever;
    through all generations my mouth shall proclaim
    your faithfulness.
For you have said, "My kindness is established
    forever";
    in heaven you have confirmed your faithfulness. R.

"I have made a covenant with my chosen one,
    I have sworn to David my servant:
Forever will I confirm your posterity
    and establish your throne for all generations." R.

"He shall say of me, 'You are my father,
    my God, the rock, my savior.'
Forever I will maintain my kindness toward him,
    and my covenant with him stands firm." R.

Zechariah his father, filled with the Holy Spirit,
    prophesied, saying:
  "Blessed be the Lord, the God of Israel;
      for he has come to his people and set them free.
  He has raised up for us a mighty Savior,
      born of the house of his servant David.
  Through his prophets he promised of old
      that he would save us from our enemies,
      from the hands of all who hate us.
  He promised to show mercy to our fathers
      and to remember his holy covenant.
  This was the oath he swore to our father Abraham:
      to set us free from the hand of our enemies,
      free to worship him without fear,
      holy and righteous in his sight
        all the days of our life.
  You, my child, shall be called the prophet of the
  Most High,
      for you will go before the Lord to prepare his way,
      to give his people knowledge of salvation
      by the forgiveness of their sins.
  In the tender compassion of our God
      the dawn from on high shall break upon us,
    to shine on those who dwell in darkness and the
  shadow of death,
      and to guide our feet into the way of peace."

Recently, at a time of prayer when many people experienced the healing power of God in their lives, as we sang
a song of praise, hands were raised in the air, voices
lifted up on high, as all together we praised the God of

heaven and earth who had come to His people and set them free, healing wounds of shame and fear, giving the grace to forgive, strengthening, pouring out His love and His blessings. It was like we couldn't help but praise, couldn't help but raise our hands and voices, having experienced the healing love of God.

Zechariah knows all about that. Right before he breaks into this hymn of praise to God, he has been healed—not only of being unable to speak, but also of self-doubt and doubt in God's power to use him. And as soon as he experiences that healing, he breaks into this beautiful hymn of praise, a hymn the whole Church prolongs every morning during Lauds.

Praise is fitting, one of the Psalms tells us, for upright hearts. Praise is fitting for those whom the Lord has set free. Praise is fitting for those who have experienced the healing love of God. Praise is fitting for those who recognize that everything they have comes from the providential hands of the Father. Praise is fitting for those who know that God has raised up for us a mighty savior, those who have been rescued.

Our hearts are made to praise. It's a good test of our spiritual health to examine our praise. When we're not praising God each day, it tells us that we're too focused on ourselves, living with too horizontal of a vision, looking too much at what is wrong. Praise lifts us out of our self-centeredness, fixes our eyes on God and His works again, reminds us that He is in control, teaches us to surrender to His goodness and to focus on His goodness.

So let's join Zechariah today in his hymn of praise. Let's bless the Lord. Let's lift our hands and heart and voice to proclaim His greatness, to praise Him for His mighty deeds, both in the history of salvation and in our own lives. Because He is God, and He deserves it.

Questions for reflection:

1. *How much of my prayer lately has been praise and thanksgiving? Why?*

2. *When has my heart been moved to spontaneously praise God? What moved it to praise?*

3. *In what situation in my life right now am I looking too much at myself? What will it mean to praise God in and from that situation?*

Action: Write your own version of Zechariah's hymn of praise, the Benedictus, praising God for what He has done in your life.

WEDNESDAY, DECEMBER 25
THE NATIVITY OF THE LORD (CHRISTMAS)
MASS DURING THE NIGHT
*"The light shines in the darkness,
and the darkness has not overcome it."*

A reading from the Book of the Prophet Isaiah (9:1-6)

The people who walked in darkness
   have seen a great light;
upon those who dwelt in the land of gloom
   a light has shone.
You have brought them abundant joy
   and great rejoicing,
as they rejoice before you as at the harvest,
   as people make merry when dividing spoils.
For the yoke that burdened them,
   the pole on their shoulder,
and the rod of their taskmaster
   you have smashed, as on the day of Midian.
For every boot that tramped in battle,
   every cloak rolled in blood,
   will be burned as fuel for flames.
For a child is born to us, a son is given us;
   upon his shoulder dominion rests.
They name him Wonder-Counselor, God-Hero,
   Father-Forever, Prince of Peace.
His dominion is vast
   and forever peaceful,
from David's throne, and over his kingdom,
   which he confirms and sustains
by judgment and justice,
   both now and forever.
The zeal of the LORD of hosts will do this!

R. **Today is born our Savior, Christ the Lord.**

Sing to the LORD a new song;
   sing to the LORD, all you lands.
Sing to the LORD; bless his name. R.

Announce his salvation, day after day.
   Tell his glory among the nations;
   among all peoples, his wondrous deeds. R.

Let the heavens be glad and the earth rejoice;
   let the sea and what fills it resound;
   let the plains be joyful and all that is in them!
Then shall all the trees of the forest exult. R.

They shall exult before the LORD, for he comes;
   for he comes to rule the earth.
He shall rule the world with justice
   and the peoples with his constancy. R.

A reading from the Letter of St. Paul to Titus (2:11-14)

Beloved:
The grace of God has appeared, saving all
and training us to reject godless ways and worldly
   desires
and to live temperately, justly, and devoutly in this
   age,
as we await the blessed hope,
the appearance of the glory of our great God
and savior Jesus Christ,
who gave himself for us to deliver us from all
   lawlessness
and to cleanse for himself a people as his own,
eager to do what is good.

In those days a decree went out from Caesar Augustus
that the whole world should be enrolled.
This was the first enrollment,
when Quirinius was governor of Syria.
So all went to be enrolled, each to his own town.
And Joseph too went up from Galilee from the town of
    Nazareth
to Judea, to the city of David that is called Bethlehem,
because he was of the house and family of David,
to be enrolled with Mary, his betrothed, who was with child.
While they were there,
the time came for her to have her child,
and she gave birth to her firstborn son.
She wrapped him in swaddling clothes and laid him in a
    manger,
because there was no room for them in the inn.

Now there were shepherds in that region living in the fields
and keeping the night watch over their flock.
The angel of the Lord appeared to them
and the glory of the Lord shone around them,
and they were struck with great fear.
The angel said to them,
"Do not be afraid;
for behold, I proclaim to you good news of great joy
that will be for all the people.
For today in the city of David
a savior has been born for you who is Christ and Lord.
And this will be a sign for you:
you will find an infant wrapped in swaddling clothes
and lying in a manger."
And suddenly there was a multitude of the heavenly

host with the angel,
praising God and saying:
 "Glory to God in the highest
 and on earth peace to those on whom his favor rests."

In all of our lives, there are places of darkness, times of struggle, areas of weakness or sinful tendencies. Maybe the darkness is from dark experiences in our past, bad things that have happened that have left their mark. Maybe the darkness is a tendency to sadness or depression or anxiety. Maybe the darkness is a temptation that we find ourselves often too weak to resist. But today, Christmas Day, the Lord says to us what the angels said to the shepherds, "Do not be afraid." He says, "The light shines in the darkness, and the darkness has not overcome it."

The light that shines in the darkness is the light of the world, Jesus Christ, the true light that enlightens everyone. That light began shining in the darkness of this world some 2024 years ago, in a simple cave in Bethlehem, when a young Virgin Mother gave birth to a little baby, surrounded by animals, watched over by her husband. And into the darkness of that cave shone the light of the world.

That light is still shining, and brighter still, more radiant than ever, brighter and brighter as each person who receives Him, receives His light, receives the power to become a child of God, and begins to walk in the light.

That light is still shining, and day by day—if we allow it to—it shines brighter and brighter in our own lives, conquering in our own hearts the darkness of sin, of shame, of fear, of death. He is Light itself, and from His fullness we receive grace in place of grace, grace to say "yes" to Him, grace to worship Him, grace to live for Him, grace to conform our lives to His, grace to share in His mission.

Today, Christmas 2024, the Light wants to shine into whatever darkness is in your life right now, whether the darkness of some wound or suffering, the darkness of a broken relationship, the darkness of illness, the darkness of your own sinfulness.

If you receive Him there—in that place of weakness—He will give you the power to live as a child of God. If you receive Him there—in that place of darkness—the darkness will not, cannot, overcome His light. And that light will shine more brightly through you, will begin to dispel the darkness in the lives of those around you.

So let's let Him in. Let's let the Light of the world pierce the darkness of our lives. Let's let the Baby Jesus be born in the Bethlehem of our hearts, as poor and unprepared, as crowded and cramped, as they may be. Let's let Him make His dwelling among us, within us, this day.

Questions for reflection:

1. *What darkness in your life has the light of Christ already overcome?*

2. *In what ways has the light of Christ shone through you to enlighten the darkness of those around you?*

3. *Where do you need Jesus to be born in your life today, to bring His light into your life today?*

Action: Light a candle in a dark room today, and repeat, "The light shines in the darkness, and the darkness has not overcome it."

THURSDAY, DECEMBER 26 (ST. STEPHEN)
*"As they were stoning Stephen, he cried out:
'Lord, do not hold this sin against them.'"*

A reading from the Acts of the Apostles
(6:8-10; 7:54-59)

Stephen, filled with grace and power,
was working great wonders and signs among the
people.
Certain members of the so-called Synagogue of
Freedmen,
Cyrenians, and Alexandrians,
and people from Cilicia and Asia,
came forward and debated with Stephen,
but they could not withstand the wisdom and the
spirit with which he spoke.

When they heard this, they were infuriated,
and they ground their teeth at him.
But he, filled with the Holy Spirit,
looked up intently to heaven
and saw the glory of God and Jesus standing at the
right hand of God,
and he said,
"Behold, I see the heavens opened and the Son of Man
standing at the right hand of God."
But they cried out in a loud voice, covered their ears,
and rushed upon him together.
They threw him out of the city, and began to stone him.
The witnesses laid down their cloaks
at the feet of a young man named Saul.
As they were stoning Stephen, he called out
"Lord Jesus, receive my spirit."

R. **Into your hands, O Lord, I commend my spirit.**

Be my rock of refuge,
a stronghold to give me safety.
You are my rock and my fortress;
for your name's sake you will lead and guide me. R.

Into your hands I commend my spirit;
you will redeem me, O LORD, O faithful God.
I will rejoice and be glad because of your mercy. R.

Rescue me from the clutches of my enemies and my
    persecutors.
Let your face shine upon your servant;
save me in your kindness. R.

Into your hands, O Lord, I commend my spirit.
Alleluia

A reading from the holy Gospel according to Matthew
(10:17-22)

Jesus said to his disciples:
"Beware of men, for they will hand you over to
    courts
and scourge you in their synagogues,
and you will be led before governors and kings for my
    sake
as a witness before them and the pagans.
When they hand you over,
do not worry about how you are to speak
or what you are to say.
You will be given at that moment what you are to say.
For it will not be you who speak
but the Spirit of your Father speaking through you.

Brother will hand over brother to death,
and the father his child;
children will rise up against parents and have them
    put to death.
You will be hated by all because of my name,
but whoever endures to the end will be saved."

It's striking, isn't it, that we go from the peaceful and beautiful scene of the Nativity of our Lord one day to the first martyr the following day? Why does the Church put things in this way? Why can't we just stay kneeling at the manger? Why must we be shaken so quickly from that quiet adoration, jolted into a world where persecution is real, where following Christ makes demands on us?

Why? Because the Gospel makes a demand on us. Because kneeling before the Baby in the manger transforms us. Because once we have adored Him, once we have received Him, once we have realized who He is and what He came to do, we are sent out on mission with Him, sent to fight to get His world back, to be, as we put it here at Acts XXIX, agents of sabotage.

St. Stephen is a perfect example of what it means to be an agent of sabotage, and his story is a powerful witness to the impact that one life lived for Christ can have.

Stephen was one of the first to follow the apostles after Christ's resurrection, and was among the first seven deacons of the Church. A man "filled with faith and the Holy Spirit," he allowed the Holy Spirit to work through him, both in his proclamation of Jesus' resurrection and in the signs and wonders he worked. His witness is so powerful, in fact, that it stirs up opposition, and, like

Christ, he is tried and falsely condemned, dragged out of the city, and stoned to death.

It seems at first like a tragic end to a brilliant life. But the death of Stephen, the first martyr, does something in the heart of a young man named Saul, who is intently persecuting Christians and who consents to Stephen's death. It is as if, through Saul's witnessing of Stephen's death, the Lord planted a seed in the hard heart of Saul, a seed that would eventually spring up to new life.

What looked like a failure in the moment, in the end was a great act of sabotage. Stephen's blood, shed for Christ, bore fruit in Saul's conversion, and Saul became St. Paul, the greatest missionary of the early church, the great apostle to the Gentiles, to whom most of us owe our faith in Christ.

The Enemy thought he was destroying a powerful witness to Christ with the death of St. Stephen. But instead, the witness of St. Stephen bore fruit in the life of St. Paul, who became himself a great agent of sabotage.

Maybe you and I won't be called to give our lives for Christ in martyrdom—or maybe we will; we don't know. But we do know that, here and now, in this time and place, the Lord has placed us and sends us out to be an agent of sabotage in our own way. And if we are faithful, we too will thwart the schemes of Satan and help bring many souls to salvation.

Questions for reflection:

1. *Who has been an agent of sabotage against the plans of Satan in your own life? What did they do? How did the Lord work through that person?*

2. *In what ways have you already seen the Lord use you as an agent of sabotage, that is to say, through you overcome some scheme of the Enemy?*

3. *What is your situation in life right now? Given that situation, how does the Lord want to use you for His mission?*

Action: Write a brief mission statement for your life, at least for your current situation, and keep it somewhere that you will see it easily throughout the week: Agent _____. Mission: _____. Means: _____.

FRIDAY, DECEMBER 27 (ST. JOHN)
"He saw and believed."

Beloved:
What was from the beginning,
what we have heard,
what we have seen with our eyes,
what we looked upon
and touched with our hands
concerns the Word of life —
for the life was made visible;
we have seen it and testify to it
and proclaim to you the eternal life
that was with the Father and was made visible to us—
what we have seen and heard
we proclaim now to you,
so that you too may have fellowship with us;
for our fellowship is with the Father
and with his Son, Jesus Christ.
We are writing this so that our joy may be complete.

Responsorial Psalm (97:1-2, 5-6, 11-12)

R. **Rejoice in the Lord, you just!**

The LORD is king; let the earth rejoice;
let the many isles be glad.
Clouds and darkness are around him,
justice and judgment are the foundation of his throne. R.

The mountains melt like wax before the LORD,
before the LORD of all the earth.
The heavens proclaim his justice,
and all peoples see his glory. R.

Light dawns for the just;
and gladness, for the upright of heart.
Be glad in the LORD, you just,
and give thanks to his holy name. R.

A reading from the holy Gospel according to John
(20:1a and 2-8)

On the first day of the week,
Mary Magdalene ran and went to Simon Peter
and to the other disciple whom Jesus loved, and told
    them,
"They have taken the Lord from the tomb,
and we do not know where they put him."
So Peter and the other disciple went out and came to
    the tomb.
They both ran, but the other disciple ran faster than
    Peter
and arrived at the tomb first;
he bent down and saw the burial cloths there, but did
    not go in.
When Simon Peter arrived after him,
he went into the tomb and saw the burial cloths there,
and the cloth that had covered his head,
not with the burial cloths but rolled up in a separate
    place.
Then the other disciple also went in,
the one who had arrived at the tomb first,
and he saw and believed.

When Peter and John run to the tomb, once they have
gone inside, they see the burial cloth, the cloth with
which Jesus' body had been covered, and the cloth from
his head rolled up in a separate place. And when they

see the empty tomb and the cloths, John sees and believes—even though, he himself points out, they did not yet understand.

Last spring, I was teaching high school theology at a local Catholic school—a lovely group of freshmen, about half of whom were Catholic (more or less practicing), and the others from other faith backgrounds, even a few atheists. In the week after Easter, I had the light in prayer that I needed to take advantage of the grace of the Octave to speak about the Resurrection with them. So we dove in, reading and discussing the Biblical witness to the Resurrection, from the Gospels and from Acts, backed up with St. Paul's certainty that if Christ was not raised from the dead, our faith is meaningless. After a couple of days, one of them, a rather skeptical nominal Catholic, said, "I just wish there were some physical evidence."

For the next class, printed in color on normal letter-sized paper, I brought in images of the Shroud of Turin, explaining in detail the evidence around it: the age of the cloth, the weave pattern, the blood stains consistent with the scourging and the crucifixion, the wounds on the head from the crown of thorns, the coins with Pontius Pilate's name over the eyes, how the image was produced—all the details I could find and easily relay to them. And then I showed them the 3D image based on the Shroud: a man in motion, in the process of sitting up. Many of them were in awe, because they had no idea that there was any extra-biblical evidence for the Resurrection. And in this day when it's hard for young people to believe without some kind of scientific evidence, the Shroud was pretty convincing to them.

But there is always a step beyond evidence, a step that each person, in his or her own free will, has to choose to take, and that step is the step of faith. There is a lot of evidence pointing to belief in God, a lot of evidence pointing to the reality of the Resurrection. But still, one has to make a choice. That choice implies a lot, because believing in Jesus Christ is not an indifferent decision. Faith in Jesus transforms us and changes our lives. It means a whole series of concrete decisions: things to let go of and things to take hold of.

C.S. Lewis once wrote that "Christianity, if false, if of no importance, and if true, of infinite importance. The only thing it cannot be is moderately important." That is to say, if this is true—if Jesus really rose from the dead—it changes everything; not just in human history, but in my own history, my past, my present, and my future.

To believe means to allow Jesus Christ, in His infinite wisdom and goodness, to change my life, to transform my whole existence. It's a risky choice, because everything is on the line. It's a risky choice, because it means letting go of everything that opposes Christ and letting Him be Lord in my life—and there are times when that will cost me. It's a risky choice, but it's worth it. Because He is alive. Because nothing on earth could ever compare to the new life He gives.

Questions for reflection:

1. *What has led you to believe in Jesus Christ and His resurrection?*

2. *What has choosing to believe in Jesus meant for your life so far? What changes has it implied for you?*

3. *What step of conversion, either of letting go or of taking up, does Jesus invite you to take today?*

Action: Spend some time today looking at an image of the Shroud of Turin, or watch a Catholic video explaining the image.

SATURDAY, DECEMBER 28 (HOLY INNOCENTS)
*"Joseph rose and took the child and his mother
by night and departed for Egypt."*

A reading from the first Letter of St. John (1:5-2:2)

Beloved:
This is the message that we have heard from Jesus
    Christ
and proclaim to you:
God is light, and in him there is no darkness at all.
If we say, "We have fellowship with him,"
while we continue to walk in darkness,
we lie and do not act in truth.
But if we walk in the light as he is in the light,
then we have fellowship with one another,
and the Blood of his Son Jesus cleanses us from all
    sin.
If we say, "We are without sin,"
we deceive ourselves, and the truth is not in us.
If we acknowledge our sins, he is faithful and just
and will forgive our sins and cleanse us from every
    wrongdoing.
If we say, "We have not sinned," we make him a liar,
and his word is not in us.

My children, I am writing this to you
so that you may not commit sin.
But if anyone does sin, we have an Advocate with the
    Father,
Jesus Christ the righteous one.
He is expiation for our sins,
and not for our sins only but for those of the whole
    world.

R. **Our soul has been rescued like a bird from the
fowler's snare.**

Had not the LORD been with us—
When men rose up against us,
then would they have swallowed us alive,
When their fury was inflamed against us. R.

Then would the waters have overwhelmed us;
The torrent would have swept over us;
over us then would have swept the raging waters. R.

Broken was the snare,
and we were freed.
Our help is in the name of the LORD,
who made heaven and earth. R.

A reading from the holy Gospel according to Matthew
2:13-18

When the magi had departed, behold,
the angel of the Lord appeared to Joseph in a dream
and said,
"Rise, take the child and his mother, flee to Egypt,
and stay there until I tell you.
Herod is going to search for the child to destroy him."
Joseph rose and took the child and his mother by
night
and departed for Egypt.
He stayed there until the death of Herod,
that what the Lord had said through the prophet
might be fulfilled,
Out of Egypt I called my son.

When Herod realized that he had been deceived by
    the magi,
he became furious.
He ordered the massacre of all the boys in
    Bethlehem and its vicinity
two years old and under,
in accordance with the time he had ascertained from
    the magi.
Then was fulfilled what had been said through
    Jeremiah the prophet:

A voice was heard in Ramah,
sobbing and loud lamentation;
Rachel weeping for her children,
and she would not be consoled,
since they were no more.

The role of St. Joseph in the story of salvation, as important as it is, is not highly visible. He was not present at the annunciation, and when he discovered that Mary, his betrothed, was pregnant, but knowing that he was not the father, he had to struggle with what to do in that situation. After wrestling with all the possibilities that he could think of, he decided to quietly divorce her, taking on himself the blame for her pregnancy, making himself look like a jerk, preserving her reputation.

And then an angel appears to him while he is sleeping, in a dream, and tells him not to be afraid, tells him the Child was conceived by the Holy Spirit. And Joseph gets up and does exactly what the angel tells him: he takes Mary as his wife, becoming her protector, leading her to Bethlehem, accompanying her when she gives birth to Jesus, loving and caring for his family.

When the angel appears to him in a dream a second time, sometime after the birth of Jesus, and tells him to get up and take Mary and Jesus and flee to Egypt, he again doesn't doubt, and he doesn't hesitate. He gets up and does exactly what the angel told him.

St. Joseph is a model of trust, a model of responding to the Lord. What can we learn from him about how to respond? First, we can learn to listen, to be attentive. The Lord speaks in many ways, through different people, and in every situation. So if we listen, we will hear Him. Second, we can learn to trust. Joseph doesn't sit around questioning the angel's messages—he receives and he puts them into action.

And that's what we can finally learn from Joseph: when we have heard the Lord, when He has told us what to do or where to go or what step to take, we need to simply do it, simply get up and do whatever it is we've discerned that the Lord is asking us to do.

Whatever the Lord is asking you to do in response to His coming this Christmas, now is the day to begin. Not tomorrow. Not later on. Not when the circumstances seem more favorable. Not when you have everything figured out, or have understood how everything is going to work. But today, now. Do as much as you have clarity to do. Take the first step and trust that He will show you the next step, as He showed Joseph. And when it was time for Joseph to move again, the Lord told him. Just as when it is time for you to move again, to take the next step, the Lord will tell you. So simply trust. And do now whatever it is that He is asking you to do now.

Questions for reflection:

1. *How does the Lord tend to speak in your life? (For example, through Scripture, in images, through certain people, etc.)*

2. *When the Lord has spoken about what to do, in what ways are you tempted to delay doing His will? What is beneath those temptations? (i.e., fear, laziness, doubt, etc.)*

3. *What is the Lord asking you to do today? When and how will you do it?*

Action: Set an image of the flight to Egypt as the backdrop on your phone or computer, and write a short prayer to St. Joseph: "St. Joseph, today help me to _____ without delay, as that is what the Lord asks of me."

A reading from the Book of Sirach (3:2-6, 12-14)

God sets a father in honor over his children;
a mother's authority he confirms over her sons.
Whoever honors his father atones for sins,
and preserves himself from them.
When he prays, he is heard;
he stores up riches who reveres his mother.
Whoever honors his father is gladdened by children,
and, when he prays, is heard.
Whoever reveres his father will live a long life;
he who obeys his father brings comfort to his mother.

My son, take care of your father when he is old;
grieve him not as long as he lives.
Even if his mind fail, be considerate of him;
revile him not all the days of his life;
kindness to a father will not be forgotten,
firmly planted against the debt of your sins
—a house raised in justice to you.

or

A reading from the first Book of Samuel
(1:20-22, 24-28)

In those days Hannah conceived, and at the end of
her term bore a son
whom she called Samuel, since she had asked the
LORD for him.
The next time her husband Elkanah was going up
with the rest of his household
to offer the customary sacrifice to the LORD and to
fulfill his vows,

Hannah did not go, explaining to her husband,
"Once the child is weaned,
I will take him to appear before the LORD
and to remain there forever;
I will offer him as a perpetual nazirite."

Once Samuel was weaned, Hannah brought him up
    with her,
along with a three-year-old bull,
an ephah of flour, and a skin of wine,
and presented him at the temple of the LORD in Shiloh.
After the boy's father had sacrificed the young bull,
Hannah, his mother, approached Eli and said:
"Pardon, my lord!
As you live, my lord,
I am the woman who stood near you here, praying to
    the LORD.
I prayed for this child, and the LORD granted my
    request.
Now I, in turn, give him to the LORD;
as long as he lives, he shall be dedicated to the LORD."
Hannah left Samuel there.

Responsorial Psalm Ps (128:1-2, 3, 4-5)

R. **Blessed are those who fear the Lord and walk in
his ways.**

Blessed is everyone who fears the LORD,
    who walks in his ways!
For you shall eat the fruit of your handiwork;
    blessed shall you be, and favored. R.

Your wife shall be like a fruitful vine
    in the recesses of your home;
your children like olive plants
    around your table. R.

Behold, thus is the man blessed
  who fears the LORD.
The LORD bless you from Zion:
  may you see the prosperity of Jerusalem
  all the days of your life. R.

or

Responsorial Psalm (84:2-3, 5-6, 9-10)

R. **Blessed are they who dwell in your house, O Lord.**

How lovely is your dwelling place, O LORD of hosts!
  My soul yearns and pines for the courts of the
  LORD.
My heart and my flesh cry out for the living God. R.

Happy they who dwell in your house!
  Continually they praise you.
Happy the men whose strength you are!
  Their hearts are set upon the pilgrimage. R.

O LORD of hosts, hear our prayer;
  hearken, O God of Jacob!
O God, behold our shield,
  and look upon the face of your anointed. R.

A reading from the Letter of St. Paul to the Colossians
(3:12-21 or 3:12-17)

Brothers and sisters:
Put on, as God's chosen ones, holy and beloved,
heartfelt compassion, kindness, humility, gentleness,
  and patience,
bearing with one another and forgiving one another,
if one has a grievance against another;
as the Lord has forgiven you, so must you also do.
And over all these put on love,

that is, the bond of perfection.
And let the peace of Christ control your hearts,
the peace into which you were also called in one body.
And be thankful.
Let the word of Christ dwell in you richly,
as in all wisdom you teach and admonish one another,
singing psalms, hymns, and spiritual songs
with gratitude in your hearts to God.
And whatever you do, in word or in deed,
do everything in the name of the Lord Jesus,
giving thanks to God the Father through him.

Wives, be subordinate to your husbands,
as is proper in the Lord.
Husbands, love your wives,
and avoid any bitterness toward them.
Children, obey your parents in everything,
for this is pleasing to the Lord.
Fathers, do not provoke your children,
so they may not become discouraged.

or

Brothers and sisters:
Put on, as God's chosen ones, holy and beloved,
heartfelt compassion, kindness, humility, gentleness,
    and patience,
bearing with one another and forgiving one another,
if one has a grievance against another;
as the Lord has forgiven you, so must you also do.
And over all these put on love,
that is, the bond of perfection.
And let the peace of Christ control your hearts,
the peace into which you were also called in one body.
And be thankful.

Let the word of Christ dwell in you richly,
as in all wisdom you teach and admonish one another,
singing psalms, hymns, and spiritual songs
with gratitude in your hearts to God.
And whatever you do, in word or in deed,
do everything in the name of the Lord Jesus,
giving thanks to God the Father through him.

or

A reading from the first Letter of St. John (3:1-2, 21-24)

Beloved:
See what love the Father has bestowed on us
that we may be called the children of God.
And so we are.
The reason the world does not know us
is that it did not know him.
Beloved, we are God's children now;
what we shall be has not yet been revealed.
We do know that when it is revealed we shall be like him,
for we shall see him as he is.

Beloved, if our hearts do not condemn us,
we have confidence in God and receive from him
    whatever we ask,
because we keep his commandments and do what
    pleases him.
And his commandment is this:
we should believe in the name of his Son, Jesus
    Christ,
and love one another just as he commanded us.
Those who keep his commandments remain in him,
    and he in them,
and the way we know that he remains in us
is from the Spirit he gave us.

Each year Jesus' parents went to Jerusalem for the
feast
of Passover,
and when he was twelve years old,
they went up according to festival custom.
After they had completed its days, as they were
returning,
the boy Jesus remained behind in Jerusalem,
but his parents did not know it.
Thinking that he was in the caravan,
they journeyed for a day
and looked for him among their relatives and
acquaintances,
but not finding him,
they returned to Jerusalem to look for him.
After three days they found him in the temple,
sitting in the midst of the teachers,
listening to them and asking them questions,
and all who heard him were astounded
at his understanding and his answers.
When his parents saw him,
they were astonished,
and his mother said to him,
"Son, why have you done this to us?
Your father and I have been looking for you with great
anxiety."
And he said to them,
"Why were you looking for me?
Did you not know that I must be in my Father's
house?"
But they did not understand what he said to them.

He went down with them and came to Nazareth,
and was obedient to them;
and his mother kept all these things in her heart.
And Jesus advanced in wisdom and age and favor
before God and man.

Often, we hear people say things like, "Well, I guess there's nothing left to do but pray," or "I guess we'll have to pray," when they don't see anything more that they can do. It's as if prayer is the last possible avenue for change, but the possibility seems so small, so we resign ourselves to throw up a Hail Mary, all the while thinking that prayer really doesn't matter much.

In the Old Testament story of Hannah, we see in her the absolute confidence in God's power even though she herself felt weak and was reproached. Her response to her own smallness, to her own shame, to her feeling weak and incapable of doing anything to change her situation, is to pray, to entrust herself and her situation to God.

But her prayer has little in common with our resignation to prayer when we've tried all other possible avenues. Her prayer comes first. She believes in the power of God to intervene in her life, to rescue her from her shame, to bring physical healing, to grant her the desires of her heart. Prayer for Hannah is not a kind of last-ditch effort, not a bit of fire insurance, but the means by which she believes that God will manifest His power in her life.

I think we don't see the power of God manifested more often because we don't really believe in His power, so we don't ask Him to work with power. Scripture tells us that, because of the lack of faith in Nazareth, Jesus was only able to cure a few sick people, not work the signs and wonders He worked in so many other places.

I know of three women in the same parish who were unable to conceive and then became pregnant and had children after asking the Lord with great faith for healing. I know of a three-year-old boy unresponsive to speech therapy and unable to talk who was healed by the prayer of a pilgrim in the Holy Land. I know a woman who was completely healed of liver cancer through prayer. I know a young adult who prayed with faith for healing from bipolar disorder and has now been living without it for three years. I have seen people go from total unbelief to adoring faith in a matter of minutes before the Blessed Sacrament.

Why does any of this surprise us? Our God became man. He walked on water. He turned 180 gallons of water into wine. He raised the dead, healed the sick, made the paralytics walk, restored sight to the blind, made the deaf hear and the mute speak. He cast seven demons out of Mary Magdalene. He died on the Cross and rose again on the third day. Nothing is impossible for Him. And everything is possible, Jesus Himself tells us, to the one who has faith.

When we pray with faith, God is able to show up in power. He has the power to do immeasurably more than all we can ask or imagine, Scripture tells us. So let's go big. Let's ask Him to do what seems for us impossible. Because nothing is impossible for God. And He wants to show us His power.

Questions for reflection:

1. *What is the "biggest" thing you have ever asked the Lord to do? What is the biggest thing you need Him to do right now?*

2. *Who in your life has a real faith in God's power, and prays with great confidence? What has the Lord done through that person's prayer?*

3. *What holds you back from asking the Lord to manifest His power more?*

Action: Spend ten minutes in prayer, asking the Lord to work with power in some area of your life or in someone else's life. If you feel like your faith is too small for this prayer, pray, "Lord, I believe, help my unbelief."

---

*"She never left the temple, but worshiped
night and day with fasting and prayer."*

A reading from the first Letter of St. John (2:12-17)

I am writing to you, children,
because your sins have been forgiven for his name's
sake.

I am writing to you, fathers,
because you know him who is from the beginning.

I am writing to you, young men,
because you have conquered the Evil One.

I write to you, children,
because you know the Father.

I write to you, fathers,
because you know him who is from the beginning.

I write to you, young men,
because you are strong and the word of God remains
in you,
and you have conquered the Evil One.

Do not love the world or the things of the world.
If anyone loves the world, the love of the Father is not
in him.
For all that is in the world,
sensual lust, enticement for the eyes, and a
pretentious life,
is not from the Father but is from the world.
Yet the world and its enticement are passing away.
But whoever does the will of God remains forever.

R. **Let the heavens be glad and the earth rejoice!**

Give to the LORD, you families of nations,
give to the LORD glory and praise;
give to the LORD the glory due his name! R.

Bring gifts, and enter his courts;
worship the LORD in holy attire.
Tremble before him, all the earth. R.

Say among the nations: The LORD is king.
He has made the world firm, not to be moved;
he governs the peoples with equity. R.

A reading from the holy Gospel according to Luke
(2:36-40)

There was a prophetess, Anna,
the daughter of Phanuel, of the tribe of Asher.
She was advanced in years,
having lived seven years with her husband after her
    marriage,
and then as a widow until she was eighty-four.
She never left the temple,
but worshiped night and day with fasting and prayer.
And coming forward at that very time,
she gave thanks to God and spoke about the child
to all who were awaiting the redemption of Jerusalem.

When they had fulfilled all the prescriptions
of the law of the Lord,
they returned to Galilee,
to their own town of Nazareth.
The child grew and became strong, filled with wisdom;
and the favor of God was upon him.

The prophetess Anna could have had a very different response to all she had lived in life. Only seven years into her marriage, her husband suddenly died. They had no living children. She had no one to care for her, no one to help her, no one to provide for her, in a culture where childless widows had little or no means for living. She had—it would seem—every reason to live in sadness, bitterness, to see herself as a victim, to blame others, to blame God.

But she didn't. Why not? Because she didn't live with herself in the center. She didn't think that her own idea about how her life should be was the standard for measuring the events in her life. She didn't set herself and her comfort and her well-being as the highest value in her life. Like the Virgin Mary, she saw herself as a creature, saw everything she received from God as a gift, knew that she had done nothing to earn any of the good she had received in her life. Certainly she suffered the death of her husband. For sure her childlessness was a cause of pain. But why focus on herself and her sufferings, when her life itself was a gift from the hands of a loving Creator, who did not abandon her when she was at her lowest?

When we put ourselves in the center, we always find something missing, always find a reason to be sad, to be frustrated, to feel like things are unfair. When we put ourselves in the center, we look down in what a good friend of mine calls "belly-button gazing," and thus turned in on ourselves, we miss so many gifts from God that He is pouring out on us each day. We miss all the blessings of the relationships that are in our lives, miss the beauty of nature. When we are belly-button gazing, we can't see the Lord when He is presented to us.

But Anna had for all these long years trained herself not to worship herself and her own well-being, but to worship God. She had trained herself by discipline (fasting) and by prayer, day and night, to wait for the Lord, to be attentive to His gifts, to offer Him worship. She had long practiced worshiping the one true God, not her own comfort, not any other source of pleasure or enjoyment or even of happiness, only God Himself, simply because He is God and thus He is worthy of our worship.

That is why, when Mary and Joseph brought Jesus into the Temple, she was able to see Him, to recognize Him, to worship Him, and to speak about Him to all who would listen. She had long ago purged her heart of every idol, and now her heart was set on Him and Him alone. So when He appeared, she could worship Him face to face, the One whom she had for all these long years worshiped in expectation.

The same is true for us. If we daily purify our hearts of our own idols (comfort, pleasure, success, our relationship with this or that person, whatever it is we tend to put in the place of God), if we day and night practice worshiping God in the interior temple of our hearts, if we practice recognizing each day all the good things we have received from Him, then on the day when He returns and takes us to Himself, we will be ready. We will recognize Him and we will worship Him, no longer from afar, but face to face, heart to heart.

Questions for reflection:

1. *Imagine being in the Temple when the Baby Jesus appears, and you recognize who He is. What happens in your heart? What things fall away in importance?*

2. *What are the things you tend to put in the center, the idols you set up in your life? What do you need to do to rid yourself of the idols?*

3. *When have you experienced true worship of God? What can you do to worship Him today?*

Action: Each time today you are tempted to look at yourself, look up and say, "Lord Jesus, I worship You alone."

TUESDAY, DECEMBER 31
*"You have the anointing
that comes from the holy one."*

A reading from the first Letter of St. John (2:18-21)

Children, it is the last hour;
and just as you heard that the antichrist was coming,
so now many antichrists have appeared.
Thus we know this is the last hour.
They went out from us, but they were not really of
   our number;
if they had been, they would have remained with us.
Their desertion shows that none of them was of our
   number.
But you have the anointing that comes from the Holy
   One,
and you all have knowledge.
I write to you not because you do not know the truth
but because you do, and because every lie is alien to
   the truth.

Responsorial Psalm (96:1-2, 11-12, 13)

R. **Let the heavens be glad and the earth rejoice!**

Sing to the LORD a new song;
   sing to the LORD, all you lands.
Sing to the LORD; bless his name;
   announce his salvation, day after day. R.

Let the heavens be glad and the earth rejoice;
   let the sea and what fills it resound;
   let the plains be joyful and all that is in them!
Then shall all the trees of the forest exult before the
   LORD. R.

The LORD comes,
  he comes to rule the earth.
He shall rule the world with justice
  and the peoples with his constancy. R.

A reading from the holy Gospel according to John
(1:1-18)

In the beginning was the Word,
  and the Word was with God,
  and the Word was God.
He was in the beginning with God.
All things came to be through him,
  and without him nothing came to be.
What came to be through him was life,
  and this life was the light of the human race;
  the light shines in the darkness,
  and the darkness has not overcome it.

A man named John was sent from God.
He came for testimony, to testify to the light,
so that all might believe through him.
He was not the light,
but came to testify to the light.
The true light, which enlightens everyone, was coming
  into the world.

He was in the world,
  and the world came to be through him,
  but the world did not know him.
He came to what was his own,
  but his own people did not accept him.

But to those who did accept him
  he gave power to become children of God,
  to those who believe in his name,

who were born not by natural generation
nor by human choice nor by a man's decision
but of God.

And the Word became flesh
and made his dwelling among us,
and we saw his glory,
the glory as of the Father's only-begotten Son,
full of grace and truth.

John testified to him and cried out, saying,
"This was he of whom I said,
'The one who is coming after me ranks ahead of me
because he existed before me.'"
From his fullness we have all received,
grace in place of grace,
because while the law was given through Moses,
grace and truth came through Jesus Christ.
No one has ever seen God.
The only-begotten Son, God, who is at the Father's
side,
has revealed him.

A few years ago, planning an outreach event on a state university campus, I invited a young woman who faithfully attended Mass, prayed daily, and came to all the campus ministry activities to take an active role in that outreach event. I still remember the look of fear that came to her eyes as she quietly stammered her response: "I...I'm...uh...I'm not sure I'm ready to come out Catholic on campus yet."

I think many of us can sympathize with her, and rather easily. It can be hard to share our faith openly, to publicly proclaim the name of Jesus, to freely tell others what He has done for us. After all, the world we live in is not exactly open, and is often rather hostile.

But we do not have to be afraid. The same Jesus who rose from the dead—the same Jesus who has overthrown the rule of Satan in our own lives to rescue us—He promises us that He gives us the power to drive out demons, to speak new languages, to heal the sick, and to face danger unharmed. He has anointed us with His Holy Spirit, filled us with His power. We have, St. John says, "the anointing that comes from the holy one."

The first disciples knew what it was like to evangelize in a hostile world. They knew what it was like to face rejection, and not just rejection, but outright persecution. But they were so convinced of the truth of Jesus' resurrection—so deeply convicted that He had come, not just to save them, but to save everyone—that they didn't hide in fear, but rather, when facing persecution, asked the Holy Spirit for still greater boldness.

You and I, we have been rescued, but there are so many people who are still there, trapped and enslaved, chained up in darkness. We can't fall prey to fear now, not when their lives are at stake, not when we have the power, given to us by the Lord Jesus Himself, to do something about it.

So let's go. Let's ask the Holy Spirit to pour Himself out on us again. Let's trust the Lord when He says that we were born for this time and this place. Let's pray for the grace to speak the Lord's word with all boldness. And let's get to the work of rescue, confident that wherever the Lord has us and to whomever He is sending us today, He has given us His anointing, His power. And nothing is impossible for Him.

Questions for reflection:

1. *Who has been an agent of the Lord's rescue in your life? Where would you be right now if that person had not had the courage to work for your rescue?*

2. *To whom in your life is the Lord asking you to witness with your testimony of rescue? Is there any hesitancy? Why?*

3. *How has the Lord rescued you? Who do you see in the same situation from which He rescued you? What will it take for you to go back in and help Him rescue others?*

Action: Invoke the Holy Spirit and then make a plan for being an agent of rescue in this new year. Begin by sharing your testimony of the Lord's rescue in your life with someone today.

ABOUT THE AUTHOR OF THE ADVENT COMPANION

Sr. Teresa Harrell is a member of the Society of Mary, religious missionary Sisters dedicated to the New Evangelization who work with the Saint John Society in their programs of New Evangelization. While in graduate school at Oregon State, she encountered Jesus alive in the Eucharist and entered the Church in 2002. She is currently serving at St. Michael the Archangel in downtown Portland, Oregon, where (among other things) she directs the Mercy Mission program. She completed undergraduate studies in English and philosophy, Master's degrees in English and Theology, and is currently working on a D.Min.

ABOUT THE CREATOR OF THE RESCUE PROJECT

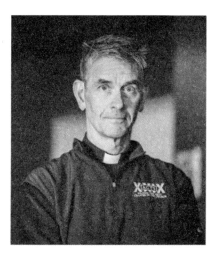

Fr. John Riccardo is a priest, author, syndicated radio host, and Executive Director of ACTS XXIX. Ordained for the Archdiocese of Detroit in 1996, he has degrees from the University of Michigan, the Gregorian University in Rome, and the Pope John Paul II Institute for Studies on Marriage and the Family in Washington, DC. He's authored numerous books including *Rescued, Heaven Starts Now, Rerouting, Learning to Trust from Mary*, and *Unshakeable Hope*.

After more than twenty years in parish ministry, Fr. John founded ACTS XXIX, an international non-profit Catholic apostolate whose mission is to renew and transform the Church by unleashing the power of the gospel, equipping ordained and lay leaders in order to mobilize the Church for mission.

ABOUT ACTS XXIX & THE RESCUE PROJECT

ACTS XXIX is a non-profit, international Catholic apostolate founded in 2019 by Fr. John Riccardo. ACTS XXIX engages in four primary missions: The  Rescue Project, reviving and equipping clergy, leadership immersives, and media creation and distribution. Please visit actsxxix.org for more information.

Launched by ACTS XXIX in 2022, The Rescue Project is a global movement that proclaims the gospel in a compelling  and attractive way. The experience creates an opportunity for people to be overwhelmed by the gospel, brought to a decision to surrender their lives to Jesus, and mobilized for mission. The series is being run in all 50 states and in over 20 countries around the world.

The eight-week video experience of The Rescue Project is intended for use anywhere—in parish ministries such as OCIA, sacramental preparation, evangelization, discipleship, men's groups, women's groups, youth ministry, and more. It can also be run in homes, restaurants, workplaces, seminaries, universities, and prisons. The Rescue Project appeals to those who have been walking with Jesus for years, as well as to others for whom Jesus is only a figure in ancient history. In other words, The Rescue Project is for everyone, everywhere, whether inside or outside the Church.

All the resources needed to run The Rescue Project are available online free-of-charge at https://rescueproject.us. Additionally, the series is available in Spanish and French, with more languages coming soon.